Comfort
Settle & Sleep

Comfort
Settle & Sleep

The natural way to care for yourself and your baby

Samantha Quinn

CONNECTIONS
BOOK PUBLISHING

To my three lovely children, Ella, Yasmin and Max.
I love you to the moon and back.

A CONNECTIONS EDITION
This edition published in Great Britain in 2015
by Connections Book Publishing Limited
St Chad's House, 148 King's Cross Road
London WC1X 9DH
www.connections-publishing.com

Text copyright © Samantha Quinn 2015
DBL system copyright © Dunstan Baby Pty Ltd
This edition copyright © Eddison Sadd Editions 2015

British Library Cataloguing-in-Publication data
available on request.

ISBN 978-1-85906-386-6

10 9 8 7 6 5 4 3 2 1

Phototypeset in ITC Stone Serif, Weidemann, Frutiger
and Snell Roundhand using InDesign on Apple Macintosh
Printed in Hong Kong

CONTENTS

introduction
Choosing the natural way

If you are reading this book, it's probably because you haven't had a good night's sleep since your baby was born. Ever since the first baby was placed into his mother's arms, parents have continued to endure sleepless nights, as one important question remains unanswered: What can be done to settle and pacify an infant?

The solution is simple, as babies really only have three basic needs, but successful results depend on patience and persistence:

1 THE INFANT'S NEED TO FEEL PHYSICALLY COMFORTABLE. Many natural methods can be used to help calm a restless baby; research has shown that regular massage can greatly reduce colic and constipation, for example, as well as other common complaints that newborns face on a daily basis. When babies feel physically comfortable they are more settled, which in turn helps promote longer and deeper sleep patterns.

2 THE INFANT'S NEED TO FEEL MENTALLY CALM. For a child to feel a sense of inner peace, a good bond has to be felt with the parent, which is created by a loving response from a parent towards the needs of their infant. A baby with a secure attachment to the parent feels safe within his surroundings, simply as a result of knowing that the parent will respond to his needs. This not only enables him to comfort himself more easily, but also optimizes the development of the nervous system, allowing the infant to respond and interact with the world around him in a healthy way. If a secure bond is not experienced, mental and even physical development can be inhibited. The child will also hanker for safety, understanding and closeness – leading to a very unsettled infant.

3 THE INFANT'S NEED FOR EFFECTIVE COMMUNICATION. Babies don't understand overwhelming feelings, and need reassurance that their emotional and physical needs will be addressed by their parents. As infants impart their needs to those around them long before they attempt to say their first word, understanding how to read your baby's cues is a vital skill you should learn in order to settle him. Babies have the ability to show several emotions, from physical discomfort and tiredness to love and contentment. If you learn to understand these cues and respond to them effectively, your infant will develop a sense of trust and form a secure attachment to you. And the best way to connect with your child, and understand his cues, is through physical contact; new babies crave – and enjoy – being touched, and, as a parent, it's the best way to nurture your newborn and express love towards him.

The power of touch

Imagine how vulnerable you would feel when seeing this big, strange world for the first time – it goes without saying that you would crave security and reassurance from those you feel safest with. For a newborn, these feelings of uncertainty are a reality, and your baby looks to you, as a parent, to make him feel protected.

During the first three months of life, your baby will quickly learn to understand the world around him in an effort to feel secure within his new surroundings. His feeling of safety is reinforced by your response to his cues and your capacity to show love and comfort through physical contact. Offering these protective and tender gestures towards your newborn creates a close and resilient bond between you, but is also of great importance in aiding the key developmental stages of an infant.

On a very primal level, babies need touch to survive. In the 1940s, studies were carried out to discover why babies placed in care were dying, despite receiving proper nutrition and being housed in a clean environment. The American psychologist Harry Harlow finally arrived at the conclusion that the only thing these infants were being deprived of was physical contact, and deduced that, to a baby, touch is critical to its very survival.

THE SCIENCE BEHIND THE PRACTICE

From Africa to Asia, Ancient Greece and Rome, massage in infant care has been routinely practised for thousands of years as a means of ensuring a healthy, happy or even fortunate child. Baby massage was only introduced to Western society in the 1970s, however, when both scientists and health professionals began to recognize the benefits that touch can bring to a newborn. These include:

- The reduction of anxiety or the stress experienced by infants after a difficult birth.
- A greater bond between parent and child.
- Enhanced physical and mental development.
- The improvement of a baby's sleep pattern as a result of increased relaxation.
- The alleviation of discomfort resulting from digestive ailments, colic and teething.
- An improvement in the overall well-being and development of the child.

Human beings have to trust in their senses in order to successfully gather knowledge about their environment; for newborns, their primary sense is touch. Your baby literally thrives on your loving attention, and it has been scientifically proven that babies who are offered plenty of physical contact at a young age are less likely to develop physical defects or mental health issues in later life.

But why does this simple act of touch reap such benefits when it comes to your baby's development? Massaging your infant stimulates the central nervous system and encourages myelination – the development of the myelin sheath in the brain. Myelin is a white fatty tissue that insulates mature brain cells by forming a sheath; this sheath ensures that the brain has a clear path to transmit messages between the neurons. Myelin sheaths play a key role in healthy brain function by creating and strengthening neural connections. This added strength ensures better development of the baby's body and brain, which in turn allows greater emotional stability and more confident environmental interaction.

To illustrate this point, Tiffany Field, a leading authority and researcher into the benefits of physical contact for infants, carried out a study on the positive effects of massage in premature babies. Field applied gentle but firm strokes to the back, neck and legs of the children and gently moved their limbs three times a day for fifteen minutes each time. Her results were astonishing, with the premature infants in the massage group gaining weight 47 per cent faster than the control group of babies who didn't receive this treatment. Additionally, the test group showed a greater development in the nervous system, had a greater level of physical activity and were more responsive to stimuli than the control group, which led to them being able to leave hospital six days earlier. In addition, the massage treatment had lasting results, as follow-up tests eight months later revealed that massaged babies did better on mental- and motor-ability tests and maintained their increase in weight.

EMOTIONAL STABILITY

Prior to labour, a baby's body is filled with high levels of ACTH (Adrenocorticotropic Hormone), which helps to prepare the baby for birth. ACTH is a cortisol hormone responsible for regulating the body during periods of stress and promoting the growth of neural pathways in the brain, but if levels of ACTH remain high, it will quickly induce negative effects such as stress, anxiety and feelings of fear. At birth, a baby's level of ACTH may be excessively high, particularly if the delivery was difficult or traumatic, but massaging the infant can help to balance out this hormone.

Feelings of emotional well-being are the consequence of a hormone called oxytocin – also known as the 'love hormone'. When a baby is massaged, this hormone is released into their system, which in turn regulates stress levels induced by the cortisol. The release of oxytocin provides the baby with feelings of security, which helps reduce periods of crying, relaxes the baby and lulls him into a slumber.

PHYSICAL WELL-BEING

One of the main reasons health professionals use baby massage is to provide relief from colic. Around 15 per cent of newborns get colic, which can be very distressing for the parent whose child is crying inconsolably, as well as for the infant experiencing the discomfort. What triggers colic isn't precisely known, but it is thought to be due to a baby's undeveloped digestive system experiencing difficulty expelling air after feeding. Massage stimulates the digestive tract, helping to strengthen it while alleviating the symptoms associated with colic, wind and constipation.

A further benefit of baby massage is its ability to aid in decongestion. A newborn's natural instinct is to breathe through his nose, and the ability to smell his surroundings helps him remain calm, as the scent of his mother is also the scent of security and reassurance. This is why babies often become agitated when congested, as the loss of their sense of smell means they can no longer recognize the scent of their mother. Their tiny nasal passages are very sensitive and prone to harbouring bacteria, which is why babies are extremely susceptible to common infections such as colds. And, as they cannot blow their own nose, they often have trouble sleeping, feeding, sucking and breathing when congested.

Unfortunately, there is no cure for a common cold, but you can make your baby feel more comfortable – and prevent the infection from getting worse – by adopting massage techniques that help clear blockages in the nasal passages. These techniques drain and soothe the sinus cavities while releasing mucus that has gathered in the chest.

Complementary therapies

In addition to massage, there are other therapies that can help, too. Aromatherapy – widely used to complement massage therapy – makes use of concentrated botanical extracts distilled from the flowers, leaves, seeds, herbs, bark and roots of plants, each naturally derived source with its own combination of active ingredients and benefits.

Successfully used as a remedy for many adult conditions with minimal or no side effects, aromatherapy has also been shown to work wonders for babies, with oils being diluted and used in aroma baby care for symptomatic relief.

Natural therapies can also work well when a baby is teething. Teething can be quite an upsetting and disruptive experience for parents, but for babies it is a painful journey full of fretful nights and a constant need for reassurance. Simply putting pressure on the baby's aching gums, for instance, helps to ease discomfort and decrease pain in the jaw caused by clenching. Reflexology can be combined with this method to great effect, helping to ease the pain and calming your baby as a result. Baby reflexology is a gentle form of natural healing that involves massaging reflex areas located on the hands and feet that correspond to areas all over the body, making it possible to treat a wide range of common infant complaints.

You will find advice on using these and other complementary therapies later on in the book.

About this book

This book is packed with effective, practical ideas and natural calming techniques to help you adjust to motherhood in a natural way and ensure your baby makes a smooth transition from the womb to the cradle.

On the pages that follow, you will discover how to read your baby's sounds and body language, so that you can give the correct response, and how to improve your baby's sleep patterns. You'll also learn how to give a full body baby massage – along with a handy 5-minute bedtime routine – to ease a number of common ailments, all presented with easy-to-follow, step-by-step instructions. Plus there's advice on complementary therapies and holistic remedies for you and your baby, ensuring that you'll both be relaxed, healthy and happy.

I have taught mothers these techniques for many years now, and with patience and persistence, I promise you this book will help you to achieve peace and contentment within your child's first year.

Samantha Quin

Understanding your baby

chapter one

From a very early age, babies communicate with the people around them using a variety of facial expressions, from frowning grumpily to delivering a thoroughly heart-warming smile. Infants also soon realize they can send signals to their parents through subtle movements of the body, turning away if feeling over-stimulated, for instance, or rubbing their eyes or pulling their ears when tired – and they will certainly let you know when their needs are not met!

These are all cues that we, as parents, begin to recognize, and the first step to reading them is to pay close attention to the nuances of your child's behaviour.

The emergence of developmental psychology has taught us the importance of raising a child with empathy, and, as you watch your baby, you will start to become more attuned to her needs, allowing you to trust your intuition, recognize your baby's signals and then respond to them accordingly.

DUNSTAN BABY LANGUAGE SYSTEM

The Dunstan Baby Language (DBL) company based in Sydney, Australia, has been carrying out infant research worldwide for almost a decade. Their studies found that babies – regardless of nationality, race or culture – typically make one of five preliminary sounds before they start to cry, and each sound means something specific. Observe your baby, and, if you hear more than one preliminary sound, pick out the one that is most frequent:

SOUND	MEANING	ACTION
'Neh' or 'nah'	Hunger	Feed the baby
'Owh'	Tiredness	Lay the baby down to rest
'Eh' or 'eh-eh-eh'	Gassiness	Burp the baby
'Eairh' (protraction of 'eh')	Gassiness	Burp the baby or deliver a short massage
'Heh' or 'heh-heh-heh' or 'ha-ha-ha'	Discomfort	Try to gauge why the baby is in discomfort and act accordingly

Crying

It can take a while for parents to fully identify the needs of their infant. When a parent understands their baby and comforts them during times of distress, it helps the infant feel secure and safe, allowing them to blossom.

If parents don't respond in a positive way to their infant's needs, this will create a fretful and stressed baby who feels unimportant. As a result, the child may become withdrawn and give up trying to communicate with its parents.

Baby's tears produce the stress hormone cortisol. When a mother is responsive to her child's cry, this stress hormone is balanced out and a sense of emotional well-being is reclaimed; conversely, if a parent doesn't respond to their child's needs, these levels of cortisol increase. If the child continues to cry for an extended period of time, rising levels of cortisol can affect developing neural pathways and the efficiency of their communication with one another, which in turn can lead to developmental issues.

KEY SIGNS THAT YOUR BABY IS EXPERIENCING UNEASINESS:

- an attempt to turn away from you
- arching their back or twisting away
- fussing and fidgeting
- closing their eyes
- dull or glassy eyes
- grabbing their hands or body
- irritability
- frantic movements
- mottling or blueness around the mouth

Recognizing the unique cadence of a baby's cry is a skill that all parents should learn in order to successfully respond to their infant's needs, as crying is a baby's primary source of communication. There are typically seven main cries that a parent will soon identify:

▶▶ THE HUNGRY CRY

Being hungry is one of the most common reasons a baby will cry, and, the younger the baby, the more likely she is to be hungry. Babies have very small stomachs, so need feeding regularly in the first few weeks of life. Before a hungry cry starts, babies usually begin displaying cues to show they're in need of a feed. As a parent, you will start to recognize your baby's unique hunger signals: most commonly, babies start to move their head from side to side, looking for something to suck. This is called the rooting reflex. If you touch the side of your

baby's head, she may turn that way expecting to be fed – another indicator that she is hungry. As more time passes, babies might try to suck their hand or your clothing, become very alert, moving their arms and legs a lot, and make grunting sounds, before delivering the high-pitched hunger cry.

▶▶ THE PAIN CRY

A pain cry can be a sudden, shrill shriek of an uncontrollable nature that can leave your infant gasping for breath. This type of cry is usually found in a baby with colic or reflux problems, attributable to an immature digestive system. Colicky babies tend to draw their legs into their abdomen, clench their fists, tense their stomachs and thrash around during crying episodes. The intensity of the pain cry is the baby's way of communicating their extreme discomfort, as well as a sense of urgency, so these cries should be addressed as soon as possible.

The primary source of pain in an infant is likely to be gassiness (colic): as a baby feeds, air bubbles can form and get blocked within the stomach and intestines, leading to excruciating stomach pain as the bubbles fail to expel themselves (see panel on page 15 for signs of uneasiness).

If your baby is suffering from trapped wind and you are breastfeeding, the first thing to do is look at your diet and eliminate potentially gassy foods. You may want to completely remove dairy and gas-inducing vegetables such as cabbage, broccoli and beans from your diet until your child stops experiencing colic, reintroducing the foods gradually in an effort to gauge their effect.

If you're bottle-feeding, try to experiment with different types of formula; comfort formulas designed for windy babies are available from a range of brands. Also ensure that the teat is the right size so your baby isn't taking in too much air with her food; anti-colic teats are particularly effective for this purpose. Always try to get your baby's wind up at certain intervals within the feeding period to help minimize the discomfort the infant may experience after a feed.

Even with the variety of anti-colic remedies currently available, some babies will still encounter difficulties in this area. The good news is that there are many different natural remedies that will help you arm yourself against the distress colic can cause your infant (see chapter 6, page 80).

▶▶ THE ILLNESS CRY

Aside from pain, your baby also has a marked cry for when she is feeling poorly. When your baby is unwell, the tone of her cry will change, as babies emit a sense of pain within a weaker, regular cry. If you think your baby may be poorly, look out for the key signs that indicate something may be wrong. Is your baby refusing to feed, or eating minimally? Is she persistently irritable? Does she appear lethargic or unusually difficult to rouse?

Is there a rise in her temperature? Nobody knows your baby as well as you do, so if you feel that there may be something wrong, consult a health professional straight away.

⏩ THE WEEPY WHIMPER

A shallow, whiny whimper can indicate your baby is bored and needs stimulating. The need for stimulus is demonstrated by the cry ceasing very quickly when the infant is picked up. You can entertain an infant easily from a young age through sensory stimulation, which can include a wide range of simple movements such as holding your baby close (touch) so she can smell your scent (smell), encouraging her to look at objects or people (sight) or hushing, singing or talking to her (hearing). Stimulating a baby's senses leads to healthy development (more about this in chapter 2).

⏩ THE ATTENTION CRY

If the weepy whimper is left unattended, it can soon turn into the attention cry. A baby that is only cuddled or soothed when they cry loudly will learn to think that this is the only way to get their parent's attention; this will lead to stressful encounters and a demanding baby. When a baby starts to whimper, it's best to try and respond to them as quickly as you can; once babies work themselves into a state, they are much more difficult to pacify. Similarly, if cues are not recognized from early on, the baby will eventually give up and make use of negative displays, such as loud crying, instead.

This doesn't mean you have to jump to attention as soon as your baby makes a squeak, but learning and observing your baby over time, and realizing what she wants, will help her to settle more easily in her new environment. Babies tend to cry less – and are happier – when they are confident their needs will be met, as a secure baby doesn't need the constant reassurance that an insecure baby requires.

⏩ THE DISCOMFORT CRY

This cry is very similar to the attention cry, though if the baby isn't giving off any direct cues it can be hard to understand what they need. If you're unsure why your baby is crying, it may be worth considering the temperature of the room – is she too hot? You can check the temperature of a baby by feeling their tummy: if the tummy is hot, remove some layers of clothing or a blanket; if it's cold, add some layers. It's also worth checking if your baby is wet and needs a nappy change, or is sore with nappy rash. If she still won't settle, she may simply want cuddling for reassurance. Don't be hesitant about showering an infant with hugs – it's impossible to give them too much love, attention or physical contact.

⏩ THE TIRED CRY

This baby cry is a soft, wailing sound, usually accompanied with cues such as rubbing the eyes, pulling the ears, yawning or generally becoming more fidgety. Learning the signs of a tired baby will help you to settle your baby at the right time before she becomes overly tired and irritable.

Reading your baby

Babies have recognizable cues – behaviours and reflexes that reflect their state of mind – whether they are hungry, tired or simply want attention. Being able to read these different signals (some obvious, some subtle) can help you provide meaningful distractions if your baby is unsettled, and gauge her needs faster, while she is more receptive to being soothed.

KEEP HER EYES ON THE PRIZE

When playing with or entertaining your baby, you may notice her eyes brightening and widening. This is your baby's way of focusing her attention on the stimulus you have provided. Whether this is a coloured ball, soft comforter or dummy, newborn children have the ability to react to the objects and people in their environment. Typically, newborns are most attentive to objects 20–30 cm (8–12 in) away, and prefer moving objects, intricate patterns and human faces. Some infants can even trace the movement of the object with their head, horizontally and vertically. Maintain eye contact with your child; not only does this enhance the rapport between you, but it also engages the baby, builds her powers of recognition and provides reassurance that your attention is fixed firmly on her.

MUSIC TO HER EARS

The sound of a familiar voice is particularly comforting to a newborn baby, and reinforces the bonding process. When you speak, you may notice that your baby shifts her gaze towards the direction of your voice. This is because a newborn's ear is particularly attuned to the frequency range of a human voice, but they also favour musical or rhythmic intonations.

PRACTICE MAKES PERFECT

It is imperative to our survival to be able to filter out 'junk' stimuli in order to pay attention to the things that really matter. Babies naturally learn from their surroundings by lessening their response to repeated stimuli (habituation) in a drowsy or sleep state; this is important in helping them to relax in their own home. This allows the household to function as normal when the baby is asleep, as well as ensuring that the infant isn't overwhelmed by their environment. All babies are different, however, and where one baby may quickly become accustomed to the sounds of a noisy home, others may take longer to habituate, and can remain unsettled. In the latter case, pay particular attention to the stimuli in the room, dimming lights or finding a less distracting place for the baby to sleep.

HUG IT OUT

When you hold your child, you may notice that she naturally adapts her form to your shape, nestling into your curves. But some children

HUNGER

Obvious cues	Subtle cues
Fussiness	Rooting
Hand-to-mouth gestures	Mouthing
Hand sucking	Turning to parent
Clenched fists	

TIREDNESS

Obvious cues	Subtle cues
Eye rubbing	Becoming quiet/still
Pulling an ear	Losing interest in stimuli
Yawning	Knotting eyebrows
Fidgeting	Small jerky movements

ENGAGEMENT

Obvious cues	Subtle cues
Smiling/reaching for parent	Brightening of the eyes
Eye contact	Raising eyebrows
Steady limb movements	
Babbling	

DISENGAGEMENT

Obvious cues	Subtle cues
Turning away	Back arching
Fussing/crying	Wrinkling forehead
Dull/glassy eyes	Frowning

prefer space, and don't like being held too close; both are normal states of being. If you notice that your baby is rigid, or thrashes in your arms, try holding her differently or finding a time of day when she enjoys a sense of closeness.

THROWING SHAPES

When awake, newborns usually move their limbs smoothly, in a rhythmic and fluid nature. They may, however, display jerkier movements for short bursts of time, but this is more to do with their underdeveloped motor reflexes than a reaction to pain, discomfort or fear.

Sleep

Babies spend a lot of their time asleep; you can expect your baby to sleep for 17–18 hours over a 24-hour period, although they don't tend to sleep for more than three or four hours at a time, thanks to a tiny stomach that needs to be fed regularly.

Your newborn doesn't understand the difference between day and night, so it's inevitable that you will have sleepless nights at the start of your baby's life. But as your infant begins to become aware of a sleep-time routine, they will become accustomed to settling in for the night. By the age of twelve weeks, most babies will sleep through a sizeable chunk of the night, with some still waking for at least one feed.

THE POWER OF REPETITION

A solid routine established at an early age will create good sleep patterns in your baby. Babies enjoy repetition – it helps them establish patterns of behaviour and provides security. Babies need repeated confirmation that things stay the same; so much is new and overwhelming for them, but repeating an activity such as a bedtime routine ensures that they learn what to expect, creating feelings of safety.

This is why repeating the same bedtime song, or reading the same bedtime story night after night, is beneficial for your child, as knowing what comes next allows the baby to start settling themselves down naturally. Repeated experience also seems to

safeguard babies against forgetting, in the same way that it takes repeated practice to master a skill. With patience and persistence, babies will respond to a bedtime routine and eventually be able to self-soothe.

THE GENTLE SLEEP SOLUTION

Sleep deprivation is one of the biggest causes of postnatal depression. A mother needs time to relax and wind down after a busy and demanding day with an infant. From as early as twelve weeks, sleep training can be incorporated into a baby's routine, to help them develop good sleep habits from an early age.

You can teach an infant that bedtime is safe and help them to relax by regulating the environment where they sleep. Lights need to be dimmed and the room quietened, with no over-stimulating colours or objects. A baby in a calm environment will be easier to settle. (For further tips on dealing with sleep deprivation, see also chapter 6.)

➡ AROMA POWER

Aromatherapy, with its natural calming properties, can form an effective part of a bedtime routine. A recent study reported that mothers who used nursery aromatherapy in their infant's bedtime routine were more relaxed, providing their child with more physical contact and positive cues (such as smiling). The mother's relaxed state helped calm their child, who in turn provided more eye contact and smiled at their mother, crying less and finally spending a greater length of time in deep sleep. Reduced levels of cortisol (the stress hormone) were also exhibited by both mother and child.

TRY IT: BEDTIME AROMATHERAPY

To disperse a calming aroma around the room where your baby sleeps, infuse the air with essential oils about half an hour before settling your baby. To do this, add 1–2 drops of lavender or Roman chamomile oil to around 500 ml (1 pint) of steaming water in a bowl. Make sure the bowl is placed away from the infant's head and out of reach of other children and animals. The steam will gently infuse the molecules of the essential oil into the room.

Aromatherapy works by inhalation, with the scent of the (diluted) essential oils stimulating the olfactory senses. The oils produce signals that trigger the brain's emotional response, resulting in the creation of mood-changing hormones. In time, the baby will begin to recognize the fragrance of the essential oils as a part of their bedtime routine (see box above).

➡➡ BATHTIME BLISS
While waiting for the oil to evaporate, you can give your baby her night-time bath. Babies often enjoy warm water on their skin, the effect of which produces the hormone oxytocin, and when oxytocin levels are raised as part of the baby's nightly routine, feelings of trust are elevated. After your baby's bath, wrap her in a warm towel and take her to the nursery to continue with her bedtime routine.

The aromatherapy teamed with a bath will result in a very relaxed child! This feeling can be enhanced by incorporating a bedtime massage: this releases yet more oxytocin, while the increased flow of blood delivers oxygen and nutrients around the baby's body, aiding a deeper, fuss-free sleep. (For more information on bedtime massage routines, see chapter 4.)

➡➡ SWADDLED AND SECURE
After the massage, dress your baby for bed and supply one last feed before bedtime. Once your baby is ready, place her in her cot, in her still awake but drowsy state. Some infants like to be swaddled to promote a sense of security, as

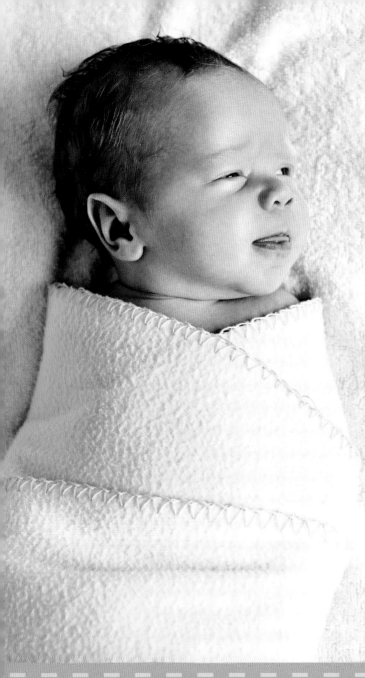

HOW TO SWADDLE YOUR BABY

1 Place your baby in the centre of the blanket.

2 Wrap one arm against her body and bring in the corner of the blanket diagonally across the body.

3 Fold the bottom of the blanket over.

4 Wrap the outer arm in and tuck the remaining blanket under her.

swaddling imitates the tight hug of the womb. This technique keeps your baby from experiencing jerky movements, which is a very common reason for night waking.

Babies are very settled by their mother's scent, so you may want to consider leaving the swaddle blanket in your bed before swaddling your baby with it. This will leave your natural scent on the material, which will reassure your child.

Once you have placed your baby in her cot, in her half-drowsy state, give her some encouraging gentle strokes. She may start to fuss at this time, as she'll be tired, but give her a chance to settle, perhaps offering a pacifier as a way of relaxing her further.

➡ ROUTINE RECOGNITION

If she still doesn't settle, give her some more reassuring touches, allowing her to see, hear, smell and feel that you are still with her. You may leave the room for a few minutes, but keep coming back, allowing her to recognize your return. If your baby moves into a real crying state, meet her emotional needs by picking her up and soothing her with close contact, gently stroking her back.

When she is calm and reaches a drowsy state again, place her back in the cot and give her gentle strokes. She will soon recognize that this is bedtime and that she is safe. And, when this is recognized, a routine will soon start to form. Repeat this routine over a period of time, and your baby will feel reassured that you will always come back if called, which helps to promote better sleeping habits and allows the baby to self-soothe.

IMPROVING YOUR BABY'S SLEEP

If your baby is still waking constantly during the night after the age of twelve weeks, it's a good idea to start a process of elimination to see if you can help to encourage a better sleep pattern.

CHECKLIST:

☐ IS YOUR BABY UNCOMFORTABLE?

A baby's digestive system is still developing at this age. If breastfeeding, you may be eating something that is disagreeing with the baby's immature digestive system. Try eliminating certain foods you eat throughout the day, to see if this makes a difference to your baby's sleep patterns.

☐ IS YOUR BABY TOO HOT OR COLD?

Babies cannot regulate their own body temperature, which is a key cause of sleep disturbance. Check the temperature of the room and the baby, by placing your hands on your baby's stomach, and remove or add blankets if necessary.

☐ IS YOUR BABY GETTING ENOUGH STIMULATION?

Babies need stimulation for healthy physical and mental development, so that they enjoy new sensory experiences. Make sure your baby has plenty of

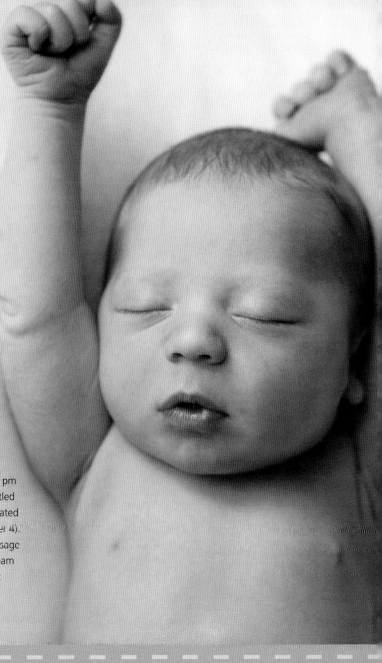

opportunities for stimulation and movement throughout the day; this will ensure her well-being, as well as help her to fall into a more relaxed sleep at night.

☐ IS YOUR BABY GETTING TOO MUCH STIMULATION?

If your baby has too much stimulation around her at night, she might find it hard to drop off to sleep. Keep the environment calm where a baby rests, and don't put any toys or mobiles near the cot. The cot should be a calm place for sleeping, not playing.

☐ IS YOUR BABY GETTING ENOUGH MILK?

A hungry baby can often be wide awake at night. Both breast- and bottle-fed babies can benefit from a feed at around 10 pm to help them sleep through the main part of the night. This is called dream feeding and, for some parents, is the best solution for wakeful nights.

Try incorporating dream feeding into your infant-care routine. If your baby is usually placed down for bed around 7 pm, then you would gently pick her up at 10 pm for her dream feed. This will help her to stay more settled during the night, especially if a massage was incorporated into the earlier bedtime routine (more on this in chapter 4). This ensures she'll stay fuller for longer, while the massage aids in the absorption of nutrients. Babies that are dream fed usually sleep until 6 am – this means around eight hours' sleep for sleep-deprived new mothers!

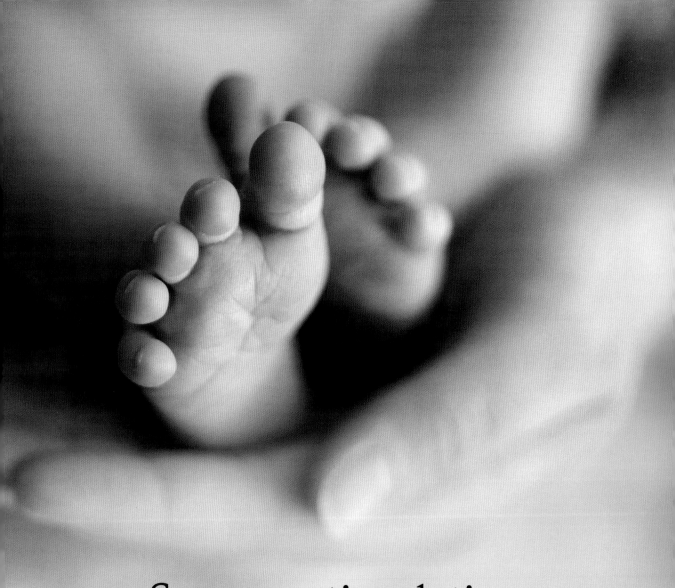

Sensory stimulation

chapter two

Billions of neurons are formed in the first stages of foetal development, allowing the newborn's brain to perform functions such as store memories, interpret sounds and acquire new skills when it is born. The only part of the newborn brain that is very developed, however, is the brain stem, which controls behaviours and reflexes such as kicking, sleeping, rooting, crying and feeding.

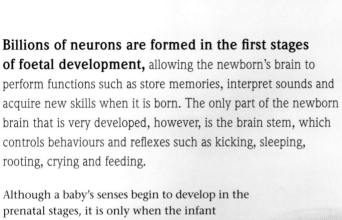

Although a baby's senses begin to develop in the prenatal stages, it is only when the infant leaves the womb that its sense organs receive the stimuli they need to mature, absorbing the fuzzy world around it in a way that marks the true beginning of the baby's sensory education.

Babies that have all their needs met through sensory stimulation will form a strong bond with their parents as a result of successful communication, and will feel more emotionally nurtured, guaranteeing a content and happy baby.

Know your audience: the key states

Just as food is imperative to the survival and growth of a child, so the brain needs sensory stimulation in order to develop. It is best to add this into a baby's routine gradually; babies are easily over-stimulated in their new environment, and prolonged activity can have an adverse effect on their mental growth. Instead, an infant will benefit more from balanced stimulation resulting from an awareness of their cues and states of being.

Studies have shown that babies go through a variety of behavioural stages and states during the course of the day. By and large, these states can be reduced down to six main types:

1 DROWSY Eyes are heavy or glazed as the baby starts to drop off to sleep. He may be unresponsive as he settles into a deeper sleep.

2 DEEP SLEEP In a deep sleep, the baby's eyes are closed and deep belly breathing will occur. He will be difficult to rouse, which often means that trying to feed a baby during this time is out of the question.

3 ACTIVE SLEEP This sleep state involves rapid eye movement (REM) sleep and the baby may make noises and move in his sleep. A sleep pattern usually consists of drowsiness followed by light sleep to deep sleep, followed by active sleep, which usually means the baby is close to waking.

4 QUIET ALERT As the baby wakes, he slowly enters his quiet alert state. Babies tend to be calm and responsive after waking, which is the best state for your baby to respond to stimuli. His face will be relaxed with bright, open eyes and a soft, calm expression, and the limbs will also be relaxed. Babies will also often return eye contact, make cooing noises and turn towards sounds in this state.

5 ACTIVE ALERT Your baby's body and face will be animated in this state, and he will be receptive to stimuli. His cues say he is happy and ready to learn about the world, which is why both quiet alert and active alert states provide the best opportunities for educating and entertaining a child. However, even though an infant's nervous system is like a sponge, absorbing this new and interesting information as best it can, prolonged stimulation can lead to the infant feeling overwhelmed. This can result in warning signs, such as the baby placing his hands over his face, sucking his hands, trying to self-soothe, assuming a foetal position, fidgeting, arching his back or neck or attempting to push away. If a parent isn't aware of – or ignores – these signs that baby needs a rest, it may not be long before the baby starts crying inconsolably.

6 CRYING The crying state results in audible cries, whimpers and sometimes screams of distress and discomfort (see chapter 1 for more on the meaning behind these cries, and how best to respond). The baby may move his body around erratically, thrashing his limbs, and may colour at the effort of doing so. In this state, all a newborn wants is to be comforted, and he will not be receptive to distractions, but as the baby gets older he will be more responsive to attempts to divert his attention away from upsetting stimuli.

Sensory play

When your baby is in a quiet alert state, try optimizing his development through different types of sensory stimulation.

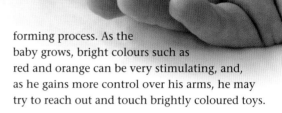

VISUAL STIMULATION

Many infants prefer looking at people rather than things, distinguishing the faces of their parents far better than other shapes and forms. By two months, a baby's sight is developed enough to visually track their parents around the room. At this age, you can begin to use sensory stimulation to entertain and educate the infant, playing fun games such as peek-a-boo, blowing raspberries or simply poking out your tongue. These visual games enhance the bonding process, as well as training and developing your baby's eye muscles.

Many high street retailers offer a wide range of stimulating baby toys that can also be incorporated into playtime. Young babies focus better on black and white, so mobiles of this colour can be hung over the changing station as a way of keeping your child settled while his nappy is changed. It's best to restrict sensory stimulation to areas where the baby is supposed to be awake; hanging a mobile over a cot can start to stimulate a baby and inhibit the settling process.

An infant should always associate different areas of the home with specific activities – for example, the floor with playtime, and the cot with falling asleep. This is all an integral part of the routine-forming process. As the baby grows, bright colours such as red and orange can be very stimulating, and, as he gains more control over his arms, he may try to reach out and touch brightly coloured toys.

AUDITORY STIMULATION

Hearing is essential for language development, and is the first sense to develop. Your baby has been listening to the sounds of the world inside your womb for nine months, which allows him to recognize and discriminate between sounds as a newborn. All manner of noises and repetition of words can help babies understand that the sounds in their environment mean something, allowing them to relate to people and their surroundings. Talking, reading, singing and humming are all great ways to excite the hearing of an infant.

TACTILE STIMULATION

When a baby is born, his sense of touch is the most developed of all the senses, and far more sensitive than that of an adult. It can therefore be seen as the most important and effective way to communicate with a baby. As we explored earlier, physical contact through massage enables you to form a bond with your child, respond to his body language and aid his physical and emotional development.

0–3 MONTHS

Responsive to:
- The newborn arrives with a well-developed sense of touch.
- Newborns have an acute sense of smell that allows them to recognize their mother's scent, and can differentiate between milk from their mother and that from another.

What you should do:
- Massage, stroke and cuddle your baby, as babies thrive on physical contact.
- Play bonding games, such as sticking out your tongue or peek-a-boo.
- Try gentle aromatherapy alongside massages or bathtime.

3–6 MONTHS

Responsive to:
- Baby will turn his head in the direction of the sound after three months.
- A wide range of motor skills is starting to emerge, such as being able to roll over or even do some baby push-ups!
- By six months, he will hear the full spectrum of sound frequencies.

What you should do:
- Talk to your child, as he can recognize your high-pitched voice from his time in the womb.
- Introduce him to rattle toys, as these will fascinate him.
- Keep offering physical contact and tactile stimulus, such as the feeling of grass under his back.

6–9 MONTHS

Responsive to:
- Baby can now sit up and support his weight with a greater measure of success.
- Taste and smell senses have begun to flourish.
- By seven months, baby can perceive a full range of colours.
- By seven months, he also gains depth perception.

What you should do:
- Babies begin to like solid foods around this age, but you may need to repeat-feed certain foods in order for your child to get a taste for them. Healthy treats may also be encouraged.
- Keep offering your child physical contact and entertain him with tactile toys.
- Educate your child through sounds and words.
- Offer him visual stimuli, as by nine months his vision will be fully developed.

The benefits of massage

chapter **three**

It is a mother's natural instinct to cuddle and caress her baby. This could stem from a primal, evolutionary urge that takes care of the infant's primary concern in its early months – its need for physical contact.

Parents in Eastern cultures have practised massage and skin-to-skin contact with babies for centuries, carrying their infants on their back or chest as they go about their day, in an effort to comfort and pacify them. (Research in Eastern and African countries has shown that close physical contact from birth results in less agressive, more empathetic adults.)

In these modern times, contact with your baby through acts such as massage reassures her that she has your undivided attention and her needs are important to you. A recent study showed that mothers who carried their baby for at least three hours a day had calmer children, in comparison to the control group, where the babies weren't carried as much. These results suggest that children who receive attention, even through simple acts such as being carried by a parent as they go about their daily tasks, have less of a need to hanker for it, and are more relaxed within their environment.

Long before babies say their first word, or even respond to us by sight or sound, they communicate and try to understand the world around them through touch. Attuned physical contact – that is, touching your baby while giving her your undivided attention – allows you both to draw upon the variety of advantages touch can bring. So, hold your baby, carry her around with you in a sling or carrier (depending on age and suitability), and sing to her every chance you get! Attachment-focused nurturing encompasses a better understanding of how integral the power of touch is to a baby's development, and a therapeutic massage can be a relaxing way of working this contact into your infant-care routine. In addition, being a new mother can sometimes feel like an endless cycle of sleepless nights, but baby massage gives you time out from feeding, changing and cleaning your child to relax and enjoy some quiet time together.

Physical benefits

● **Stimulates the digestive system** Babies are born with an immature digestive system, as it takes roughly three months for the digestive tract to fully develop, which may explain the sudden reduction of colic when a baby reaches this age. Massage helps to break down trapped wind lodged in the baby's stomach; the repetitive motion relaxes the muscles, helping them tone and develop while stimulating the colon. This eases the baby's bowel movements, preventing the pain and discomfort caused by constipation.

● **Helps development of premature babies** Research shows that premature babies have been seen to gain more weight, have better sleep patterns and are discharged from hospital sooner, compared to premature babies who do not receive massage.

● **Promotes good health** Regular massage can keep a child healthy, thanks to its encouragement of efficient homeostasis, or inner balance, and can promote the healing of common complaints such as congestion, catarrh, digestive problems, restless sleep, earache and teething.

- **Aids circulation** Massage aids the baby's circulatory system, increasing the flow of oxygen and nutrients around the body.
- **Stimulates internal organs** Massage stimulates the baby's organs, promoting their development.
- **Improves nourishment, promoting better sleep** Massage can help low-birth-weight babies to experience faster weight gain, as it increases the baby's appetite while also encouraging the release of enzymes that digest food. This leaves the baby better nourished and fuller for longer, which in turn promotes a deeper and longer sleep at night.
- **Strengthens the immune system** Massage encourages the development of the respiratory system, which increases the oxygen uptake that can help strengthen the baby's immune system.
- **Guards against infection** Massage and regular movement promotes the flow of lymphatic fluid, improving the baby's resistance to infection.
- **Promotes touch** Touch is just as important as a nourishing diet, and is essential to the healthy growth and development of your baby. Babies who are deprived of touch do not thrive.
- **Increases growth hormones** A regular massage encourages the increase of growth hormones from the pituitary gland.
- **Improves joint flexibility** As muscles relax, they allow the free movement of the body's joints. Baby massage encourages muscular relaxation and joint flexibility, which promotes a wide range of physical movement. This releases stress and tension, which can cause physical discomfort in a baby.

Emotional benefits

- **Promotes stronger bonding** Eye contact, physical contact, smiles, laughter, the sound of your voice or soothing music, the baby's ability to smell your scent – all add to the act of communication between you and your child.
- **Encourages trust** These early instances of trust, as a consequence of regularly massaging your child, lay the foundation for the interactions your child will have with other adults. A trusting child is likely to be happier and more confident in social situations than one who rarely receives physical contact.
- **Relieves anxiety** By easing muscular tension, massage calms the emotions and relieves any trauma or anxiety associated with the birth and transition from the womb. Babies delivered through C-section, or who have had a traumatic birth, can benefit enormously, as massage helps reduce the production of cortisol (stress hormones) in the baby's system.
- **Promotes body awareness** Massage gives your baby a greater awareness of her own body, which encourages a sense of spatial orientation; babies that are massaged demonstrate better physical ability.
- **Promotes relaxation** The relaxation and mental well-being a child gains from massage will allow them to spend less time fretting and more time developing and learning.
- **Induces feelings of well-being** Massage stimulates the release of endorphins – the body's natural feel-good hormones. Coupled with the reduction of cortisol, this induces general feelings of well-being throughout your baby's body.

Benefits for you

- **Eases breastfeeding** Massaging your baby enhances the secretion of prolactin, essential for milk production, easing the process of breastfeeding. Breastfeeding also encourages the bonding process, and the release of oxytocin during the act helps to relax both you and your baby.
- **Promotes feelings of well-being** If you suffer from depression, the act of massaging your child can promote feelings of well-being within yourself, particularly over time, as you watch the benefits that it brings to the development of your baby.
- **Strengthens the parent–child bond** The relationship of a baby to its parent is strengthened through the production of oxytocin – the 'love hormone' – during massage (the simple act of implementing massage techniques in an infant-care routine can help mothers suffering from postnatal depression achieve a closer bond with their baby).
- **Helps you understand your baby** Massage allows you to observe your child's body language, creating a greater understanding of your baby's cues.
- **Enhances bonding between father and child** Research has shown that fathers who massage their child for fifteen minutes on a daily basis are more confident with their infant and experience better interactions with them. In addition, a massage from the father (or other caregiver) allows the baby to learn that these adults can offer them physical and emotional support too.

Massage preparation

There are a number of factors that need to be considered when it comes to massaging your baby.

CREATING A CALMING ENVIRONMENT

When introducing baby massage into your routine, choose a specific area in your home in which to carry it out. Babies love repetition, and they will soon associate the area with feelings of well-being created by the massage. Ideally, pick a place in the nursery, if possible, as this will couple the infant's feelings of relaxation with the security of a familiar space. If you can, carry out an early evening feed before your baby's last feed; this will help her absorb the food better while also promoting deeper sleep.

Your chosen area should be warm (around 24°C/75°F), as the baby will be undressed for the full benefit of skin-to-skin contact, and babies lose heat at a greater rate than adults. Check for draughts, especially if you're carrying out the massage on the floor, and ensure that your baby is resting on a comfortable surface, such as a soft warm towel or blanket.

Creating a calm atmosphere is essential in helping to soothe and settle your baby. You might like to play gentle instrumental background music, or infuse the air in the room

with the light fragrance of essential oils (see page 22). If the massage is carried out in the evening (or on a darker afternoon), try dimming the lights or lighting a candle, but be careful to keep any naked flames at a safe distance and height from the baby. Peace and quiet is crucial, so choose a time when you can turn off the television and relax together without interruption. Good preparation will create the best environment for your baby, which in turn will help calm, settle and soothe her.

USING CARRIER OIL

If you're using oil as part of the massage, be sure to check that it's suitable for your newborn's sensitive skin. The oil needs to be fragrance-free, just in case your baby ends up ingesting it (for instance, by putting her freshly massaged hands in her mouth). It is also advisable to avoid nut oils in case of an allergic reaction, and mineral-based

oils, which aren't easily absorbed and can leave a residue that is sticky, greasy and slippery.

The best oils to use are organic, unrefined vegetable, avocado or grapeseed oils, as these cause the baby no discomfort if ingested (see table below). Carry out a patch test on your baby, to ensure that her sensitive skin does not display any signs of irritation from the oil. Simply place a small amount on the wrist or ankle and keep an eye on the area for around thirty minutes; if a reaction occurs, wash the skin immediately and use different oil.

GETTING COMFORTABLE

It's important that you, as the masseuse (or masseur), are seated comfortably before the baby is massaged. Make sure that your back is sufficiently supported in a comfortably padded chair, or, if you're sitting on the floor, prop yourself against a wall, perhaps with a couple of cushions or pillows for support.

As the routine continues, you will intuitively adopt a position of natural comfort that will suit both you and your child.

TYPE OF OIL	PROS	CONS
Sunflower	• Non-greasy • Contains vitamins A, D and E, which can be beneficial for children with skin conditions • Has an antibacterial effect on the skin of premature babies • Suitable for all skin types	• Short shelf life, especially if stored in well-lit areas
Grapeseed	• Cold-pressed grapeseed oils are odourless • Contains vitamin E and linoleic acid • Suitable for all skin types	• Can be expensive
Avocado	• Perfect for sensitive or dry skin, especially when used with a base oil such as sunflower • Very nourishing, containing vitamins A, B and D, and fatty acids	• Can become sticky if used by itself • Has a fairly strong odour
Vegetable	• Cold-pressed vegetable oils ensure the natural properties of the oil are preserved • No sticky residue • Odourless	• Be mindful of not buying a 'contaminated' oil (i.e. one that isn't cold pressed) • Can be expensive

When not to massage

While massage can certainly enhance your infant's feelings of well-being, contribute to her physical health and help relieve many common complaints, it is not a form of medical care.

If you ever feel that something could be medically wrong with your child, or if you know that she is ill, seek advice from a health professional. If your child has a medical condition, check with your doctor before adding massage to your infant-care routine (see right).

In addition, there are some illnesses or general health conditions where massage should not be used. Do not massage your baby if they have:

● **A fever** – a fever will increase the baby's heart rate and a massage can decrease it. To be safe, wait until the fever goes away completely to continue with the routine.

● **Diarrhoea** – massaging the tummy will ease the release of stools. If your baby has diarrhoea, their loose stools will most likely increase with a massage.

● **Any rashes or lesions on the skin** – an inflamed skin rash can be irritated with a massage, while open sores can become infected.

● **Been immunized within the last 48–72 hours** – a vaccine is meant to be absorbed by the body at a certain rate, and, since massage stimulates the lymphatic and circulatory systems, a massage could increase the possibility of an unwanted reaction.

CAUTION

The following is a list of medical conditions that must be taken into account before massage can be considered for your infant. If you have any concerns, make sure you seek the advice of a medical practitioner.

Do not massage your child if they have recently experienced or are experiencing:

- An infectious disease
- A fracture, sprain or swelling
- A haemorrhage
- Jaundice
- Meningitis
- Childhood leukaemia
- Osteoporosis/brittle bones
- An operation
- A congenital heart condition
- Aortic valve stenosis
- Atrial septal defect
- Pulmonary valve stenosis
- Ventricular septal defect
- Congenital dislocation of the hip
- Down's syndrome
- Dysfunction of the nervous system
- Epilepsy
- Asthma
- Skin allergies
- Cuts and bruises
- An unhealed navel

Baby massage

chapter four

Massage techniques

At its most fundamental, the key to a good massage is an effective technique. This can be achieved by maintaining constant physical contact with your baby, keeping a steady rhythm and flow; by breathing deeply to allow yourself to relax; and – above all else – by enjoying this time to bond with your baby.

There are four main types of massage stroke that ensure an effective technique:

➡ CONNECTING STROKES
➡ EFFLEURAGE
➡ PETRISSAGE
➡ FRICTION

CONNECTING STROKES

Connecting strokes are used at the beginning of a massage session to help your baby to relax, making him aware that your time together is beginning. These strokes are long and continuously flowing, using a light touch to cover your baby's body while pausing briefly on the joints to induce a sense of relaxation. They may also be used to signal the end of the massage, too.

EFFLEURAGE

'Effleurage' is a French term meaning 'a light touch'. This stroke involves a long, soothing action using the flat of your hands or fingers. After you have performed the opening connecting strokes, effleurage can then

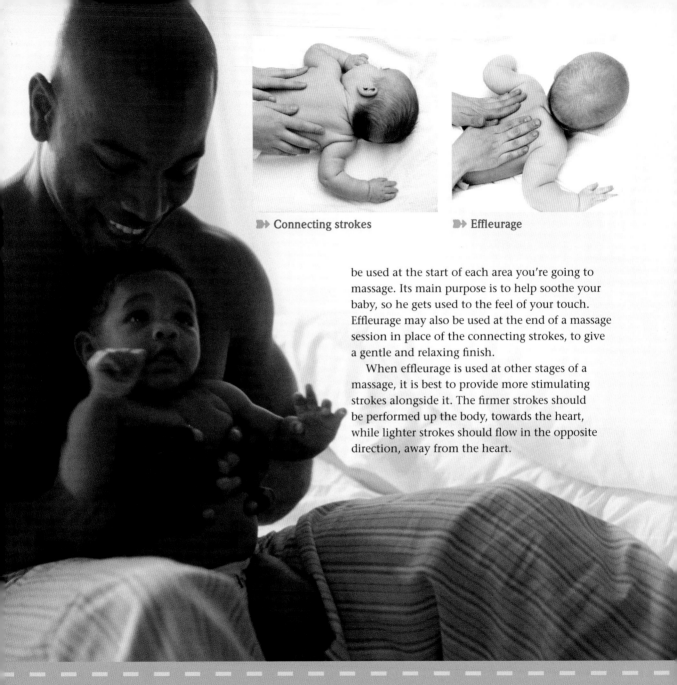

Connecting strokes

Effleurage

be used at the start of each area you're going to massage. Its main purpose is to help soothe your baby, so he gets used to the feel of your touch. Effleurage may also be used at the end of a massage session in place of the connecting strokes, to give a gentle and relaxing finish.

When effleurage is used at other stages of a massage, it is best to provide more stimulating strokes alongside it. The firmer strokes should be performed up the body, towards the heart, while lighter strokes should flow in the opposite direction, away from the heart.

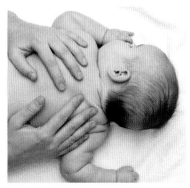
▶▶ Kneading

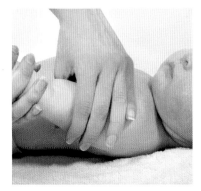
▶▶ Wringing

▶▶ Friction

PETRISSAGE (KNEADING AND WRINGING)

Such words conjure up images of bakers vigorously pounding dough amid clouds of flour, or washerwomen from a bygone age energetically twisting and squeezing water from dripping clothes. Needless to say, petrissage is not quite so extreme or physical, especially when it comes to massaging your baby! These are probably the most important massage strokes you will be using, as they encourage blood circulation and the removal of waste products from the muscles.

▶▶ KNEADING

When massaging little bodies, a lighter kneading action should be used. Place one hand flat on your baby's skin and lightly squeeze and fold the flesh underneath, then release as you repeat the action with your other hand. Imagine you are softly kneading dough, and rock from hand to hand as you work over a specific area, keeping both hands in contact with your baby throughout.

Kneading is especially useful for releasing tension in the legs when your baby has been in a car seat or buggy for a substantial length of time.

▶▶ WRINGING

Imagine your hand action when wringing something out: your hands move in opposite directions, in a twisting action. Perform this technique in a gentle, continuous motion, moving slowly over a specific area. The aim is to work on releasing tension in larger areas of your baby's body, such as the legs.

FRICTION

Although this form of stroke is usually used to relieve muscular tension, friction can also be very beneficial for relieving trapped wind and breaking down air bubbles in your baby's digestive system. This stroke involves using your thumb or fingertips to apply slight pressure to particular areas, paying attention to how your baby reacts to see where it's having the most effect.

The massage routine

Once you and your baby are comfortable and relaxed, breathe deeply. Every massage session should begin with you asking your baby's permission to commence the massage, so that he starts to recognize the cue.

So, before you start, warm your hands and, while doing so, make eye contact and ask aloud,

'Would you like a massage, baby? Are you ready?'

This act of asking permission shows respect for your baby and, even though infants can't respond verbally, they will begin to recognize the preliminary ritual to a massage. Asking permission will make you more sensitive to baby's mood and help you identify your baby's readiness through his bodily cues. Understanding and communicating with your baby via his non-verbal signals helps to establish positive communication, which in turn helps to form trust and promote feelings of security.

After asking the question, take a few moments to watch your infant carefully for the communication cues that indicate if it's okay to proceed (see right).

TO BEGIN

When baby is happy and ready to receive a massage, place a small drop of oil in your hand and warm it in your palms (make sure you have enough oil to glide over his skin smoothly and easily). Start with a connecting stroke (see page 41) before the massage sequence begins, to relax and comfort your baby: place the palms of your hands on your infant's body and stroke him gently from shoulders to hands, back to the shoulders, down the side of the stomach, down the legs and back to the shoulders again. This is a lovely introduction to the massage, calming baby and easing the tension out of his muscles.

The following pages include a complete massage routine covering head to toe, but you can perform each section as an individual massage, too. There's also a 5-minute bedtime routine that you will find invaluable (see pages 62–5).

INDICATIONS THAT YOUR BABY IS READY FOR A MASSAGE:

- Still and smiling
- Gleaming eyes and bright face
- Smooth movement of arms and legs
- Cooing, babbling and other mouth sounds
- Wide-open eyes
- Eye contact
- Hands in the mouth
- Grasping for objects or for you
- Cuddling
- Playful wiggles

Legs

A leg massage is a great way to relax your baby. Babies love their legs being touched – it calms their nervous system by soothing their sensory nerve endings as well as encouraging the release of comforting hormones such as oxytocin. When oxytocin levels are raised, feelings of trust are elevated, leaving a calmer, more contented baby. Work through all the steps on one leg first, then move across to the other.

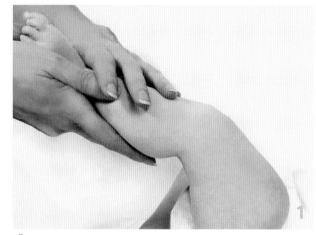

1 Support the left leg under the ankle with one hand. To help relax the leg, raise it slightly from the floor, still supporting the ankle joint, and give the leg a relaxed bounce. *Look at your baby and softly say,*

'Relax, baby, relax; relax, baby, relax.'

Supporting your baby's ankle with the palm of one hand, sweep up and down the leg with a gentle effleurage stroke using your other hand, alternating hands as you go. Repeat several times. Be sure to use gentle pressure gliding down the leg, to avoid putting any undue stress on the valves in the veins.

Legs *continued*

2 Securing the ankle joint with one hand, use your other hand to knead up the leg using your fingertips and the pad of your thumb, taking care not to put any pressure on the knee joint. Gently glide your hand down the back of the leg to the ankle and repeat a few more times.

This movement is great for lymph drainage, and will really help build up your baby's immune system.

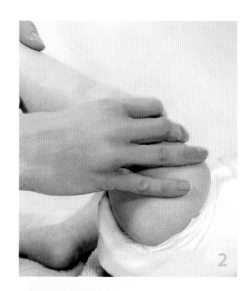

3 Place both hands softly around the calf, then gently glide your hands up the leg in a wringing action, as if gently wringing out a cloth.

This helps to release pent-up tension in this area. Again, avoid putting any pressure on the knee joint or twisting the knee when performing this technique.

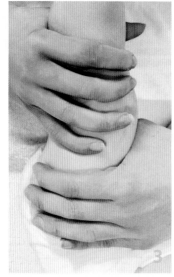

4 Place one hand flat on your baby's thigh and lightly squeeze and fold the flesh underneath using the kneading technique, releasing as you repeat the action with your other hand. Rock from hand to hand as you work over the thigh, keeping both hands in contact with your baby throughout.

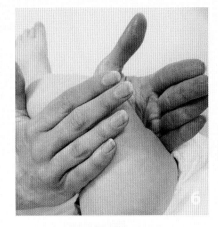

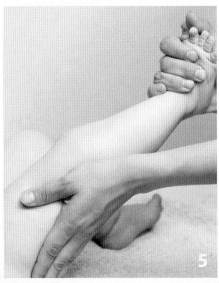

6 Hold your baby's thigh between the palms of your hands and roll the thigh so that your palms are moving in opposite directions. This stroke is excellent for relieving that last bit of tension in baby's thighs, and for promoting body awareness.

You can have fun with this technique, singing a jolly song as you go, as babies love the sound of Mummy's voice. Try:

'Jelly on a plate, jelly on a plate, wibble wobble, wibble wobble, jelly on a plate.'

5 Gently elevate your baby's leg, then softly sweep up the leg from ankle to thigh using an effleurage stroke, gliding smoothly using one hand after the other.

This technique is very soothing for babies and helps circulation.

Feet

Now we can move down to the feet. When massaging your baby's feet use firm pressure, as little feet become quite tickly! Work through all the steps on one foot first, before moving across to the other, and remember to keep your hands oiled up.

1 Allow your baby's foot to relax into the palm of your hand. Put the pad of your thumb under the big toe and, with a gentle but firm pressure, glide around the base of the toe.

Repeat three to four times.

2 After this movement, glide the pad of your thumb down to the centre of the foot and make small circular movements in a clockwise motion.

This area stimulates the vagus nerve (responsible for facilitating normal digestion and metabolism in the body), and is greatly beneficial for any kind of digestive complaint (see also reflexology techniques in chapter 5, page 68).

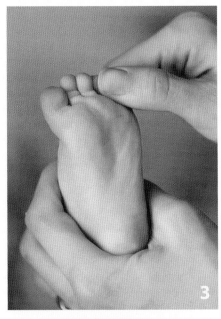

3 Cradle your baby's foot and, taking one toe at a time, gently roll each toe between your thumb and index finger, starting at the base of the toe and working up to the tip.

You could recite a little nursery rhyme as you go:

'This little piggy went to market ...'

This technique can help with teething pain, as it works on the reflex point for the teeth (see also chapter 5, page 69).

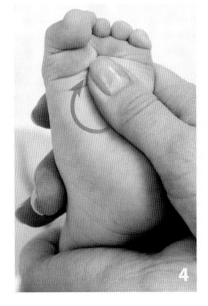

4 With your baby's foot resting in your palm, wrap your hand gently around the foot to secure it. With your other hand, use the pad of your thumb to make circular movements in the centre of the sole, just under the ball of the foot.

This is excellent for calming and settling your baby, as it works on the solar plexus reflex point (see chapter 5, page 69) and releases oxytocin into the baby's system.

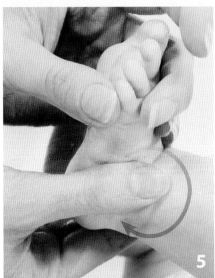

5 To finish the foot massage, raise your baby's leg slightly off the floor and secure the ankle. Using the thumb and index finger of your other hand, gently glide circles around the ankle joint.

This movement encourages flexibility and muscle tone, as well as being very soothing.

Tummy & chest

Massaging your baby's tummy is a great way to support his digestive system. If your baby is suffering from complaints such as colic, wind, reflux or constipation, a little tummy massage can really soothe these troubles. The abdomen is very sensitive, however, and your baby may cry if hands are placed on an area where trapped wind has formed. Distracting him with singing, chatting or even talking about your day can help him relax, as he will be settled by your voice.

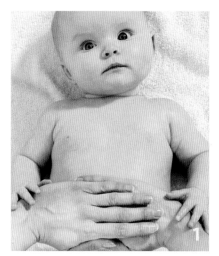

1 Rest your hands on the tummy for a few seconds to relax the abdomen.

This will bring warmth to the area, helping to comfort your baby and relax the intestines, allowing any trapped air to be released (trapped air in the intestines is one reason for prolonged crying in babies).

2 With your hands still placed horizontally across the tummy, begin to 'paddle stroke' in a downward motion using alternating hands.

This soothing stroke will help relax the whole tummy area (the stomach is said to be the centre of our emotions, so keeping the tummy relaxed will keep baby relaxed).

3 Hold your baby's legs at the ankles and gently elevate the legs off the floor. Repeat paddling strokes on the tummy with one hand to help release trapped air lodged in your baby's bowel.

This technique also stimulates the digestive tract, helping to tone and mature the digestive system, thus combating colic.

Lower the legs back down, allowing any trapped air to be released.

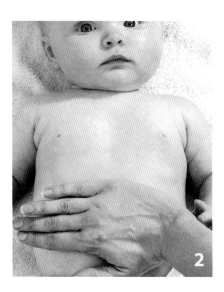

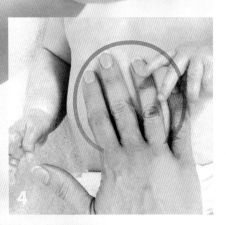

4 In a clockwise motion, stroke the pads of your fingertips gently around the tummy.

This helps glide the air bubbles around your baby's digestive system, effectively dispersing them. NOTE: Only massage in a clockwise motion, as this is the direction in which the digestive system flows.

5 Continuing this clockwise motion, place one hand on top of the other and make long sweeping circles around baby's belly.

This stimulates the digestive tract while helping to tone and develop the stomach muscles.

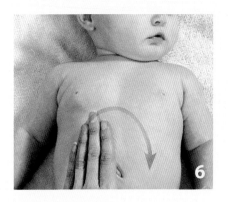

6 Using your fingertips, gently glide an upside-down 'U' shape clockwise over your baby's stomach to encourage the digestive system some more.

7 Now imagine your baby's tummy is a clock face. Place your hand on number 9 and draw a crescent moon shape clockwise to number 5, then take over with your other hand to perform a deeper stroke, drawing a big sunshine (circle) around the tummy.

This is a slightly deeper stroke than the tummy circle (step 5), and is really beneficial for working trapped wind through the bowel area. Stimulating the area with both hands aids circulation, and is excellent for constipation, as it helps with softening stools so they can be passed easily.

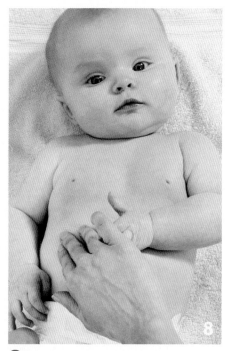

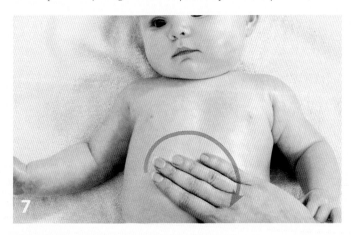

8 Using the pads of your fingers, dance them all over your baby's tummy, pressing them gently into the flesh one at a time in a sweeping manner. Use all four fingers to swipe these gentle presses on baby's tummy.

This helps break down the last of any of those painful air bubbles left in the system.

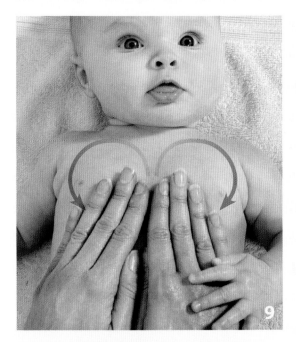

9 Ensuring you still have enough oil to glide over the skin easily, move onto the chest. To help relieve chest congestion, place your hands in the centre of the chest and draw a heart shape by gently moving up the chest towards the shoulders.

Aid the bonding process as you make the heart shape by making eye contact with your baby and saying, 'I love you'.

Repeat five times.

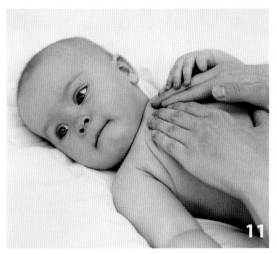

10 To promote a better night's sleep and relieve congestion, place your hands on the centre of your baby's chest and draw several criss-crosses ('X' shapes), alternating your hands as you go, working towards the shoulders then back to the centre.

11 Finally, make butterfly movements (mini rocking movements, like butterfly wings fluttering) over the chest area with the palms of your hands, to help break down congestion even more.

This stimulates the lymph nodes, helping with lymphatic drainage, removing the waste products within your baby's system and keeping minor illnesses at bay.

Arms & hands

Babies love their arms being touched,
and a soothing arm massage will help to induce
feelings of calmness, thanks to the release
of endorphins – the body's natural feel-good
hormones – and comforting hormones
such as oxytocin. As with the leg massage,
work through the whole routine on one
arm, before moving onto the other.

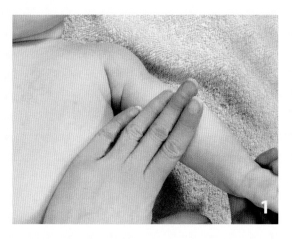

1 Gently hold your baby's arm and bounce it slightly to ensure it's relaxed. When ready, stroke from the elbow to the shoulder, then around underneath the armpit and down the side of the chest. Repeat the stroke around six times. This is a sensitive area, so firmer pressure is advised.

This technique is excellent for helping with lymphatic drainage.

2 Supporting your baby's wrist with one hand, massage from the wrist to the upper arm using rhythmical strokes (such as the effleurage technique used on the legs; see page 47). Use long, gentle strokes to relax the baby.

This soothes the sensory nerve endings and calms the nervous system.

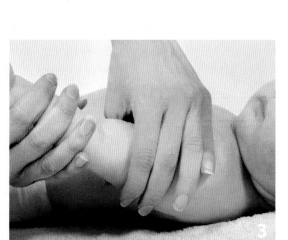

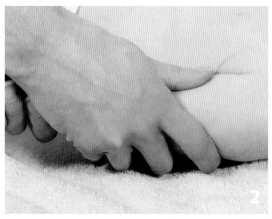

3 Place your hands either side of the wrist and gently wring upwards, towards the upper arm, as if very delicately wringing out a cloth (don't use any pressure on the elbow).

Babies can build up a lot of tension in their arm muscles during the first months of life, and the wringing technique really helps to release this and relax the arms, as well as being excellent for body awareness.

4 Moving onto the hand, take one of your baby's fingers and gently roll it backwards and forwards in very small, slow movements, gradually working through each finger in turn.

You can use musical rhymes with this technique, such as:

'Tommy Thumb, Tommy Thumb, where are you? Here I am, here I am and how do you do?'

Repeat for Peter Pointer, Toby Tall, Ruby Ring, Baby Small and, finally, Fingers All. This technique is good for the circulatory system, and helps encourage motor skills.

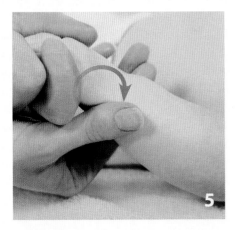

5 Securing your baby's wrist with the pad of your finger and thumb, gently glide little circles around the wrist joint.

This brings nutrients and blood flow to the joints, which aids flexibility and muscle tone.

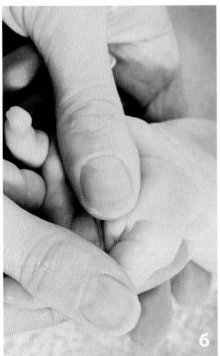

6 Now massage inside your baby's palm to stimulate the solar plexus reflex point (see also chapter 5, pages 68–9).

This helps to promote well-being and relaxation.

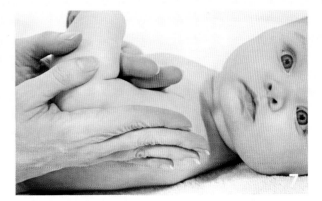

7 Supporting your baby's arm, gently glide long rhythmical strokes towards the body.

These strokes work with the heart, boosting circulation.

Face

Facial massage is especially good for relieving teething pain. Use only a very small amount of oil (or none at all) when massaging the facial area, and only use your fingertips.

1 Without blocking your baby's view, make a triangle over his head with your thumbs, gently placing your thumbs on the eyebrows near the bridge of the nose, and glide outwards along the eyebrows to open up the brow line. Repeat several times.

This technique is excellent for relieving tension from teething headaches, or if a baby has been crying inconsolably.

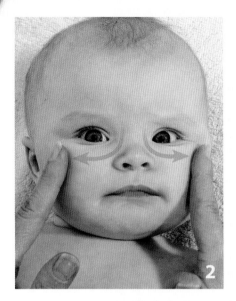

2 To massage your baby's sinuses, place your fingertips either side of the bridge of the nose and gently glide up and down the nostrils. Then slide your fingers under the eye area, around the back of the ears and along the jaw line, finishing at the chin. Repeat several times.

Massage both sinuses at the same time to release mucus, ease soreness and clear congestion. This helps drain all the nasty mucus away through the lymph nodes, helping baby to breathe more easily.

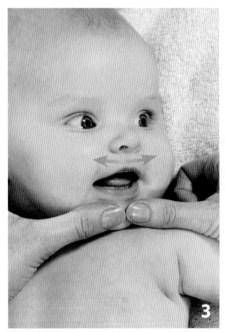

3 In one long stroke, run your fingers across the top lip and up under the nose, then out in opposite directions towards the ears. Using your thumbs, repeat this from the centre of the chin towards the ears. Repeat several times.

Putting pressure on your baby's gums helps to relieve teething pain and the discomfort teething brings.

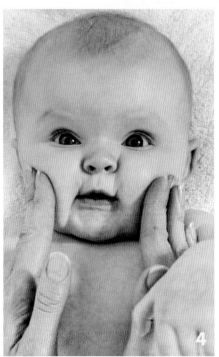

4 Use your fingertips to gently make small circles around your baby's cheeks where there is a small dip.

This helps to release any tension in the jaw, and further relieves the pressure of teething.

THE MASSAGE ROUTINE 59

Back

Regular massage of the back will encourage strong posture and muscle tone in this area, which in turn will promote overall balance.

> ## CAUTION
> Never massage, or put any pressure directly on, the spine itself, as this delicate human framework is extra-fragile in the immature body of a baby.

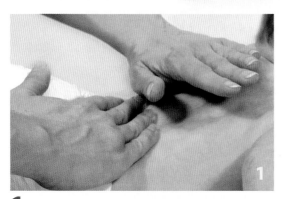

1 Position your baby on his stomach (this aids the strengthening of the spine). Place your palms horizontally and glide them down your baby's back, gently moving them back and forth in a paddling motion, down towards your baby's bottom.

This type of paddling technique helps to relax tense muscles and releases oxytocin, which makes the baby feel good.

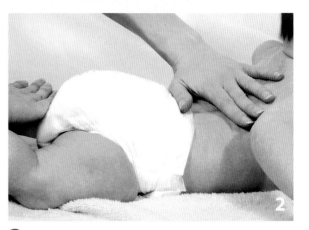

2 Now extend the paddling movement downwards in long rhythmical strokes, from the top of your baby's back gently down to his feet.

This technique helps infants to develop body awareness.

3 Placing the pads of your thumbs either side of your baby's spine, draw little circles from his bottom up to his neck, massaging the muscles either side of the spine.

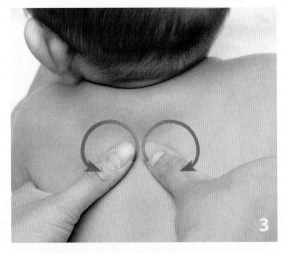

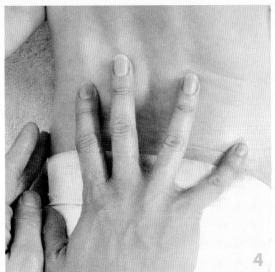

4 For the final closing movement, split your fingers like a comb and fan down either side of baby's spine in long rhythmical strokes.

As the massage comes to an end, the strokes can become lighter and slower. You can also add a final connecting stroke to signal the massage is over, by sweeping down across baby's shoulder blades, down the arms, down either side of the spine, down the backs of the legs and off the toes.

When the massage is finished, wipe any excess oil off your hands before picking up your baby. Wrap him in a towel or blanket and give him a well-deserved cuddle.

5-minute bedtime-massage routine

Establishing a bedtime routine is the key to instilling good sleep habits in your baby. A calming routine that follows a predictable pattern every night helps give your baby the cue that it's time to put her little head down to rest, which in turn helps her to settle more easily.

What's more, a bedtime routine is a wonderful way to bond with your baby at the end of a long day. After all, time spent snuggling, singing lullabies and quietly reading is the closest, calmest time you'll get to spend with your infant.

Massage can be very beneficial for helping babies to sleep more deeply and for longer periods of time. This means you, as a parent, being able to sleep longer, too – hopefully all night! Not only does massage help your baby to release the stress that builds daily from the stimuli that create new experiences, it also allows her to relax and enjoy this special quiet time.

GETTING READY

Firstly, prepare a relaxed environment – make sure the room is warm enough and that the lights are dimmed. You might also like to try lightly vaporizing essential oils around the room, away from the baby, to aid relaxation (for more on this, see pages 21–2).

Begin to talk to your baby in a calm voice and smile at her. This will help to stimulate her senses and make her feel more comfortable and content. As before, always ask permission to massage your baby, saying aloud, 'Would you like your bedtime massage now?' Wait for baby's answer (see box on page 44), responding appropriately to her cues while warming the massage oil in your hands by rubbing them together (again, ensure your hands are well oiled, to glide over baby's skin freely and easily). This will help your baby to recognize another cue that it's time with Mummy.

At bedtime, you want to focus on using relaxing effleurage strokes. It's important not to over-stimulate at this time, so relaxing strokes and calm lullabies are best. While carrying out the massage, continue to make eye contact to make sure your baby is comfortable and enjoying the experience. If you're happy singing or telling stories, go ahead, as your baby will be drawn to the sound of your voice. Whatever makes you both feel relaxed will work for you and your baby.

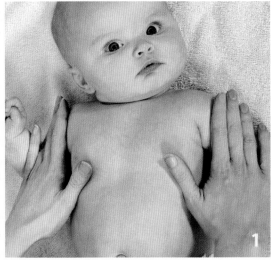

1 Start by placing your warmed hands gently on the top of your baby's chest. Use the connecting (effleurage) stroke to sweep gently up the shoulders, across the arms and back up the shoulders again. Continue by gliding your palms down the sides of the tummy and down the front and sides of the legs, then softly sweep your hands back up the sides of the stomach to rest lightly on the chest. Repeat six to eight times.

2 Now use your palms to slowly and lightly make criss-cross movements over the chest.

This movement is great for easing congestion and aiding deep breathing, which promotes better sleep.

3 Next, move down to the tummy. Using both hands, smoothly sweep clockwise in a circle movement. Repeat six to eight times.

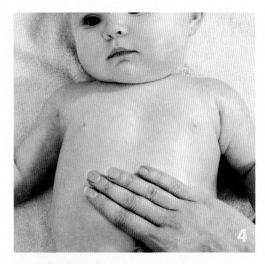

4 Placing the pads of your fingertips on your baby's belly, make little circular movements around the tummy area, ensuring that movements are small and slow.

This helps to break down air bubbles in the digestive system, so your baby isn't racked with gassy pain at night.

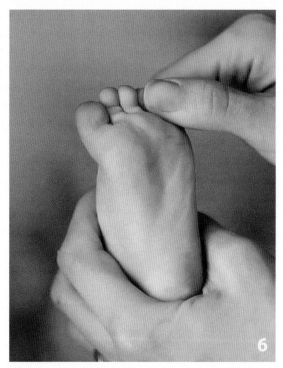

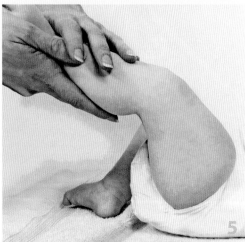

5 Using both hands, gently effleurage up and down your baby's legs with the palms of your hands, alternating legs as you go.

6 Slowly massage the bottom of your baby's foot and make toe circles with each toe, singing quietly:

'This little piggy ...'

To finish, kiss the foot – babies really love this! Repeat on the other foot.

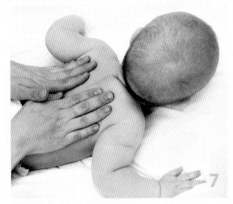

7 Turning your baby over, gently massage her back, starting from the shoulders and stroking over the bottom and down the legs, taking extra care not to put any pressure on the spine.

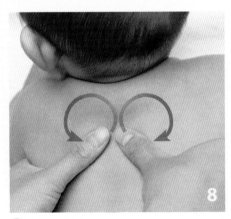

8 Continue stroking the back a few more times, before placing your thumbs either side of the spine and gently making circles in an upward motion, along the spine.

The back massage will help to calm the nervous system and release oxytocin into the body.

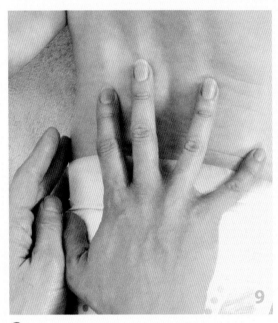

9 Finish off the bedtime routine by gently stroking down your baby's back with your fingertips, avoiding the spine.

Complementary therapies
& holistic infant-care solutions
chapter five

Complementary therapies can offer natural calming techniques to soothe and settle your baby, as well as helping to alleviate common ailments. Some of the most beneficial therapies for babies are outlined below.

Baby reflexology

Effective and safe, reflexology is based on the principle that parts of the feet (or hands) correspond to different parts of the body, and that stimulating these 'zones' can release tension or help relieve pain caused by illness.

According to reflexologists, energy from the point that is touched is transmitted across a network of nerves from the feet to other parts of the body (such as the stomach – great for helping colic; or the back – ideal for soothing the nervous system), sending messages from the brain to sensory and motor nerves throughout the body, creating a calming and comforting effect.

Babies are particularly responsive to reflexology, thanks to the underdeveloped arches on their feet and their fairly soft skin and bones; many mothers will instinctively rub their child's feet and hands when they are cranky, crying or uncomfortable. By applying gentle pressure to congested areas in the feet, blockages can be released to restore the flow of energy to the whole body.

Because it can be used on the move, as well as constituting a complementary practice alongside massage, reflexology has quickly gained popularity among the parenting community – especially for those times when your little one is proving difficult to soothe in a busy supermarket! It's easy to learn, with no need for prior preparation, and only a few minutes of reflexology are required to get results.

REFLEXOLOGY MASSAGE ROUTINE
Using reflexology on a daily basis can really help to heal your baby's body by detoxifying, relaxing and balancing it, helping to detect and even treat imbalances before your baby experiences any symptoms. The following routine can be used every day in its entirety, or just use each section as and when needed, even when you're on the move.

Always begin reflexology by rubbing your hands together to warm them before handling your baby's feet (there's no need to use any oil for a reflexology

massage). Remember, this is a special and fun time for you and your baby, so sing, talk and just relax.

To begin, support your baby's feet with his heels in your palms. Hold them loosely, so he can move his feet away if they start to become over-sensitive. Keep your strokes soft, as babies are very responsive to this touch therapy.

Digestive complaints

This technique stimulates the vagus nerve, which supplies the nerve pathway to the heart, stomach, liver, pancreas, spleen, small and large intestines and gall bladder. It facilitates normal digestion and metabolism in the body, so is greatly beneficial for any kind of digestive complaint. The final movement, where you glide your thumb towards the centre of the foot, addresses the stomach's reflex point, which, when stimulated, is excellent for maturing and toning the digestive system, helping to relieve colic, reflux and constipation.

1 *Support your baby's foot in the palm of your hand.*

2 *Place the pad of your thumb around the rim of the big toe and, with a gentle but firm pressure, glide around the base of the toe. Remove your thumb and repeat five to six times.*

3 *Now glide the pad of your thumb down to the centre of the foot and make small circular movements in a clockwise motion.*

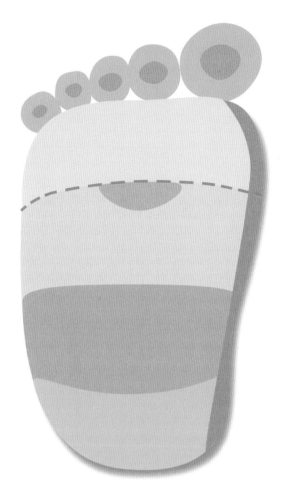

- head/teeth area
- sinuses
- solar plexus
- upper abdominal area
- lower abdominal area
- pelvic area
- spine reflex area
- -- diaphragm

Soothing and settling

This area represents the spine, which houses the central nervous system, transmitting messages from the brain to sensory and motor nerves throughout the body. Stimulating this area calms your baby; it is an excellent reflex point to use if your baby has become over-stimulated throughout the day.

1 *Rest your baby's foot in the palm of your hand and place the thumb of your opposite hand on the big toe.*

2 *With a firm touch, glide your thumb softly along the outside of the foot, ending at the heel.*

3 *Return to the top of the big toe and repeat four to five times.*

Colds and congestion

This technique will help to release congestion and soothe your baby's sinuses. These movements are very beneficial for babies in general, as babies are nasal breathers from birth, and often become easily congested due to increased bacteria in the nasal cavity.

1 *Place your finger and thumb pad on your baby's little toe and use a squeeze-and-release pressure to break down any clogged-up mucus (the sinus reflex points are located up the back and sides of the toes).*

2 *Repeat along each of the toes.*

Promoting better sleeping patterns

This technique works on the solar plexus reflex point, which is a network of nerves situated just below the diaphragm – a useful area to consider when seeking to calm your child. It's an excellent technique for parents on the go, as it releases oxytocin into the system, helping your baby to relax and settle if he becomes fretful when in public.

1 *With your baby's foot resting in your palm, wrap your hand gently around the foot to secure it.*

2 *Using the pad of your thumb on the opposite hand, make circular movements just under the centre of the diaphragm line.*

Teething

End your massage by working on the teeth reflex – this technique is important when your baby is going through his teething period. The reflex point for babies' teeth is found on the front of the toes, below the nail.

Securing your baby's foot in your palm, press up each toe with your other hand. After finishing each toe, rotate the toe once in a clockwise motion, reciting the nursery rhyme 'This little piggy went to market' as you go.

Homeopathy for babies

Practised worldwide for more than two centuries, this gentle yet effective system of alternative medicine uses only natural ingredients such as minerals, plant extracts, salts and oils, administered in highly diluted form, in an effort to kick-start the body's natural healing process.

The first study into the benefits of homeopathy for children was carried out in Nicaragua in 1994, on eighty-one children with acute diarrhoea. The study showed that children who received homeopathic treatment recovered 20 per cent faster than the control group who received a placebo, suggesting that homeopathy played a role in speeding up the healing process.

Homeopathy addresses your child's energy levels and emotional needs, while also stimulating their immune system. One of the advantages of using homeopathic remedies in infant care is that they are palatable; they can be easily dissolved on the tongue, and have a light, inoffensive taste. What's more, professional homeopaths are usually attentive to the needs of the child, ensuring that the child is free to speak or act without judgement. This is thanks to their professional ethos that information is as much gathered from observation as it is from the verbal account of the parents. This non-clinical approach to needs of the infant can help to ease anxiety and assure infants that their emotional needs are being addressed in addition to their physical well-being.

CAUTION

Homeopathy is an effective complementary therapy, but should not be seen as an alternative to medicine. When your child is ill, it's imperative to remain vigilant when it comes to the development of their symptoms and their level of discomfort. If you have any reason to believe that your child may be getting worse, seek medical attention as soon as possible. For acute or severe illnesses, seek the advice of your GP. You should also seek advice from a trained homeopath before giving remedies to your child.

HOLISTIC TREATMENT SOLUTIONS

CONDITION	SYMPTOMS	CAUSES	TREATMENT
Nappy rash	• Soreness or redness on the baby's bottom or around the genitals • Dry or itchy rash • Blistering of the skin • Scaly skin	• Irritant chemicals released from baby's excretion • Allergic reaction to topical applications such as moisturizing lotion or other cosmetic products • Unsuitable washing detergent	• Create a mild solution of calendula and hypericum and wash the baby's bottom in it. Follow with the application of calendula cream. Keep the area thoroughly clean by changing the nappy regularly. *See also page 88*
Teething approximately 6 months to 3 years old	• Irritability • Stomach complaints • Fever • Sore gums	• Baby's milk teeth are beginning to come through	• If the infant is not lactose intolerant, alleviate teething pains by dissolving two Combination R tissue-salt tablets on the tongue three times a day at feeding time. • For acute pain, give two tablets dissolved in warm water every 15 minutes. *See also pages 95–6*

> **Caution:** Always follow the treatment instructions on the packet and seek advice from a professional homeopath before giving to your infant.

CONDITION	SYMPTOMS	CAUSES	TREATMENT
Colic, gripe and reflux starts at approximately 3 months old	• Discomfort • Irritability • Inconsolability • Distended stomach • Pulling up of the legs	• Causes of colic are not definitively known, but the child's symptoms could be attributed to trapped air in the digestive system	• Make some simple changes to your infant care routine *See pages 80–82 and 92–4* • Massage is a beneficial practice in addressing intestinal complaints *See pages 50–53*
Irritability and inconsolability	• Continuous crying • Screaming		• Use organic teas such as chamomile to calm your child. Boil the tea and let it cool to lukewarm. Serve 30 ml (1 fl oz) doses three to four times a day.

Aromatherapy for babies

Aromatherapy is often praised for its ability to create a sense of calm, but less is known about its powerful yet gentle capacity to heal. For babies suffering from minor complaints or disorders, aromatherapy can provide some efficient solutions that can be used time and time again.

Essential oils tend to be potent in their concentrated form, so should only be applied to a baby's sensitive skin using a carrier: by diluting the oils in water and using carrier oil as a base, you can ensure the aromatherapy solutions you use will be suitable for the delicate skin and excitable senses of your child.

There are a number of essential oils that can be used to provide relief from common ailments, but the ones most widely used for infants are listed in the table opposite (NOTE: eucalyptus and peppermint should not be used on babies under the age of three months):

USEFUL AROMATHERAPY TREATMENTS
➡ BUMPS AND BRUISES
As children begin to explore the world around them, they may often pick up some bruises and bumps along the way.

ESSENTIAL OIL	USES
Tea tree	Antibacterial, antiseptic and astringent properties.
Roman chamomile	Calming and effective against minor skin complaints such as eczema; can also provide asthma relief and help to ease sprain injuries.
Eucalyptus	Decongestant with antiseptic and antibacterial properties
Peppermint	Aids digestion and can be used to treat insect bites.
Mandarin	Relieves digestive weakness with uplifting effect.
Frankincense	Antiseptic, cytophylactic (cellular regeneration) and calming properties.
Lavender	Best known for its calming properties, lavender oil also has anti-fungal, antibacterial and anti-inflammatory benefits that make it suitable for treating a wide range of common ailments.

Symptoms: Discolouration of the skin, bumps that are sensitive to touch.

Causes: Knocks and falls.

Practical steps: Gently rub the bruise to get the blood flowing into the injury and, if necessary, apply a cold compress.

Aromatherapy treatment: For the cold compress, sink 2–3 drops of lavender oil into 300 ml (½ pt) ice-cold water, mix well and douse a flannel in the mixture. Hold against the skin for 10 minutes. For a topical ointment, combine 3 drops of helichrysum with 3 drops each of lavender and frankincense oils, then blend with 30 ml (1 fl oz) grapeseed oil. Smooth the oil liberally onto the affected area.

⮞⮞ TEETHING

Teething usually occurs when a child is between six and twenty-four months old.

Symptoms: Irritability, swollen gums, flushed cheek on one side, tendency to chew or suck things.

Causes: The emergence of the baby's first set of teeth.

Practical steps: Teething rings, particularly those that can be chilled in the fridge, provide a great way of cooling down sore gums while addressing the child's rooting reflex. Teething gels will be readily available at your local pharmacy, and most contain a mild local anaesthetic that helps to ease discomfort.

Aromatherapy treatment: Add 5 tbsp of sweet almond oil to a small mixing bowl, adding 1 drop each of lavender and Roman chamomile oils to the mix. Stir well and rub a small smear (2 drops or less) along your child's jaw, from ear to ear (be careful to avoid the eyes, mouth and cheekbones). To help soothe a child's fretful mood, try placing a vaporizer (a bowl of hot water containing 1–2 drops Roman chamomile or lavender oil) in their room, in a corner far away from them.

CAUTION

If you are unsure before beginning treatment, address any concerns or questions with a qualified aromatherapist. As with every natural remedy mentioned in this book, ensure that you seek medical attention if your child suffers from any of the following:

- Fitting or convulsions
- Aversion to light
- Severe diarrhoea or vomiting
- Prolonged bouts of coughing
- Serious headaches
- Prolonged loss of appetite
- Long bouts of crying/screaming due to pain
- Fever of 38°C/101°F and above
- Refusal of feeds

⮞⮞ MINOR SUNBURN

The remedy given here is suitable for children over the age of twelve months. For children under twelve months, seek medical attention if they get sunburnt, as the condition can be more serious than it initially appears; as always, it's best to err on the side of caution.

Symptoms: Pink, tender skin after sun exposure.

Causes: Sun exposure.

Practical steps: Hydrate the child by giving them plenty of fluids – preferably drinks with a high water content – and keep them out of the sun.

Tepid baths can also be effective – just be careful to pat the skin dry gently afterwards. For topical relief, aloe vera creams for infants are readily available in pharmacies and can be used to ease the pain of a burn.

Aromatherapy treatment: For a soothing spray that can be used to treat minor sunburn on unbroken skin, sink 2 drops of lavender oil into 300 ml (½ pt) water and shake well. Spray the affected area as required.

Music therapy

Music is renowned for its power to diminish the stresses of the day, and a baby's ability to wind down to some choice tunes is no different to our own!

Sound plays an important role in the development of a child in the womb, preparing it for the world outside, and studies have shown that babies can respond to music even within their mother's body. Some studies even offer the argument that a child can gain a cognitive advantage from listening to classical music – a phenomenon known as the 'Mozart effect'. Other researchers have found that children who learned to play an instrument for six months did better at spatial tasks and were more effective problem-solvers.

Whether these studies have a point or not, it is an indisputable fact that, when a baby is born, he experiences an orchestra of sounds – from the music that flows out of the radio as mum goes about her day, to the sound of dad's voice, to the upbeat tracks and sound effects that come from toys and books. The world is alive with the sound of music, so why not complement your infant-care routine with your own playlist?

THE SOUND OF SINGING

Try playing classical or instrumental music to your child, being careful to keep the volume at a low level so as not to damage his sensitive ears. Or you could hone your karaoke skills by singing to him! Whether you think you sound like Celine Dion or Daffy Duck, studies have shown that the most effective sound for newborns is the sound of a parent singing to them, as babies love the rhythmic lull of a nursery rhyme and the familiarity of mum or dad's tone. Babies don't care about the quality of your voice – they simply love to hear the sound of the most important people in their world.

If you'd feel more comfortable speaking than singing, then do so; any vocalization is important to young babies. Keep up a quiet chatter as you massage your baby, and feel the bond between you strengthen.

Craniosacral therapy

Labour is a stressful experience for both mother and child. The physical exertion and consequent surge of chemicals from the experience can turn the warm, safe environment your baby has grown accustomed to into an inner sanctum of chaos and confusion.

As a result, your child may bring his feelings of shock and trauma from the labour into the world with him, symptoms which manifest in conditions such as colic, sleeplessness and constant fretting.

Craniosacral therapy works on the premise that there is more to the body's rhythm than just the pace of its breath and its heartbeat, proposing instead that life expresses itself through constant movement. The bones of a baby's skull – particularly after a difficult birth – may not be able to resume a normal position after being compressed or subjected to forceps, which means that blood flow to the brain or nerves may be compromised. By very gently manipulating the skull, craniosacral therapists seek to shift the bones back into place, releasing pressure and encouraging healthy brain development. They also help promote and alter the flow of cerebrospinal fluid, which in turn helps to stimulate the body's natural ability to heal and regulate itself, thus relieving the infant's stress and anxiety associated with the birth. Consult a professional if you'd like to explore this therapy further for your child.

Common ailments
in babies

chapter six

In a world swarming with bacteria and viruses, babies emerge from the protection of the womb as something of a blank canvas for infection, disease and sickness, so it's no wonder they are more prone to ailments and complaints than adults. Not only is their immune system desperately trying to develop, but their little bodies are busy adapting to the new processes of breathing and feeding, which can quickly result in problems with their digestive and respiratory systems.

Thankfully, many of these conditions aren't too serious, but whether suffering such seemingly small ailments as coughs and nappy rash, or more severe ones like fevers and vomiting, no one likes to see their baby unwell. While this chapter is not intended as a comprehensive medical guide, it outlines the common ailments and complaints your baby may face in the first weeks and months of life outside the womb, with advice on how you can provide natural solutions and remedies to offer your child relief.

On the pages that follow, you will find guidance on:
➡ COLIC
➡ COLDS AND COUGHS
➡ FEVER
➡ CRADLE CAP
➡ ECZEMA
➡ NAPPY RASH
➡ CONSTIPATION
➡ DIARRHOEA
➡ GASTRO-OESOPHAGEAL REFLUX (GOR)
➡ TEETHING
➡ SLEEP DEPRIVATION

DON'T DELAY

If you are in any way concerned about your baby's health, contact your doctor or other healthcare provider as soon as possible.

Colic

While colic is a fairly common condition, affecting roughly three in ten babies under the age of five months, it can be very unsettling for both parents and their babies.

For the most part, infants suffering from colic may appear completely healthy apart from succumbing to recurring periods of prolonged and unsoothable crying. The standard used by doctors is the 'three threes': if your baby is crying for at least three hours a day, at least three days a week, for at least three weeks, colic is probably the issue.

That said, three weeks enduring long bouts of crying can seem like an eternity, and a distressing one at that, because there's no obvious reason for the crying, and usual attempts to soothe your baby are mostly ineffective. Even when she does begin to settle, the cries may suddenly start again without apparent cause, in a cycle that can last several hours, before sleep finally claims your exhausted infant.

At other times, your baby will appear completely fine with no adverse signs, and, over time, the attacks of colic will occur less frequently, until the digestive system has matured and developed.

CAUSES AND SYMPTOMS

The term 'colic' is derived from the word 'colon', as it was originally thought this ailment was caused by abdominal pain in the lower intestine. Various other theories now abound as to the cause, however, including: hormone levels that affect the muscles in a baby's gut; the immaturity of a baby's digestive system, which gradually gets used to feeding within a few months; and that colic is simply an extreme form of normal crying. The last is true in as much as colic does not appear to be a disease or illness itself, but, in addition to the 'three threes', babies with colic may exhibit the following symptoms:

- Excess crying during the evening, especially after or during feeding, or crying that begins at the same time each day
- Sudden, high-pitched crying that the normal methods of soothing do not settle, resulting in your baby falling asleep exhausted
- A drawing-up of the legs, as if suffering from stomach pains, and the tummy may be swollen

---

CAUTION

Take your baby to the doctor if you suspect she has colic, to rule out any more serious underlying causes. This is especially critical if there are any of the following complications:

- Fever (temperature in excess of 37.5°C/100°F)
- Vomiting, constipation or diarrhoea
- Crying that sounds like your baby is in pain rather than mere discomfort, as this could indicate something more serious, such as an injury
- Your baby is over four months old, as the digestive system should no longer be causing signs of colic
- Your baby is not gaining weight and has no appetite

- Clenching hands into fists and curling toes
- Passing wind or faeces that may result in your baby calming down, as if relieved
- Facial flushing and paling with the effort of crying
- Arching of the back

NATURAL SOLUTIONS AND REMEDIES

Hopefully, apart from colic, your baby will be pronounced healthy by the doctor, leaving you free to work out a strategy to help her (and you) get through this difficult time. While there is no cure for colic, try the following, to see which help to ease your baby's suffering (make sure you also take the time to look after your own health, as having a colicky baby can be very stressful):

- **Feed your baby little and often** to help her digestive system cope and get used to eating, keeping her upright so she doesn't swallow too much air.
- **Try experimenting with your diet** if you are breastfeeding, as there are a number of foods that can have an adverse effect on infants (for example, spicy food, garlic and onions, caffeinated food and drink, citrus fruits, cabbages and cauliflower).
- **Wind or 'burp' your baby often,** especially after feeding.
- **Try soothing your baby with motion or sound,** such as a vibrating baby seat or taking her out

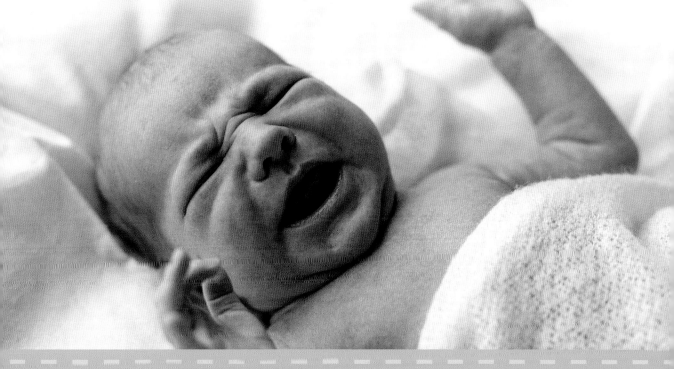

in the car, or playing 'white noise' or seating her near a running washing machine.

- **Hold your baby close to your body** to calm and comfort her when she is going through a bout of crying – don't offer her stimulation.
- **Try massage,** as this can help to relax a baby's abdominal muscles (see pages 50–53).
- **Try baby reflexology** to break down the air bubbles in the digestive system (see page 68).
- **Consider taking your baby to a chiropractor,** who can help with pains that relate to the nervous system and troubles with the digestive system.
- **Try herbal remedies,** such as giving your baby a couple of teaspoons of fennel water (simmer a teaspoonful of fennel seeds in 500 ml/1 pt water for 10 minutes and allow to cool) every 15 minutes or so. If you're breastfeeding, it's worth drinking herbal teas such as chamomile, fennel and lemon balm, as their soothing elements will be passed on to your baby and will help settle her digestive system.
- **Bath your baby in warm water with a drop of lavender essential oil.**
- **Try homeopathy:** Chamomilla (chamomile) is recommended for babies suffering from colic (before giving your baby a homeopathic remedy, please seek guidance from a qualified professional).

Colds and coughs

Babies' immune systems are still developing and learning to battle the various bugs and colds that pollute our atmosphere. Add to this the natural predilection of infants to explore and experiment by picking things up and shoving them in their mouths, without any regard to health and hygiene, and it's no wonder that colds and coughs are all the rage in parenting.

CAUSES AND SYMPTOMS

There are over two hundred different types of cold, which no doubt contributes to the fact that babies seem to suffer an endless succession of them! Coughs often go hand in hand with colds, though if your baby's cough shows no sign of going away, or gets worse at night or after play, it's worth going to see your doctor to rule out the possibility of a chest infection or asthma.

No doubt you are already pretty familiar with the symptoms of colds and coughs. Coughs are fairly self-explanatory, while colds often reveal themselves in the following ways:

- A running or blocked nose
- Frequent sneezing
- Crying may sound more hoarse than usual
- Occasionally may be accompanied by a fever (see page 84)

CAUTION

If your baby is showing signs of having difficulty breathing, or her cold symptoms have lasted for more than ten days, take her to see the doctor, as infants tend to be more susceptible to complications such as chest infections.

NATURAL SOLUTIONS AND REMEDIES

Your baby's mouth, nose and eyes are an ideal breeding ground for bacteria and viruses, and, while we are still yet to find an effective cure for these microscopic adversaries, most of them clear up within five to seven days, thanks to your baby's natural defences. During this time, there are plenty of ways to help make your baby more comfortable and happy, when suffering from the obligatory coughs and sniffles:

● **Increase the humidity in your baby's room** using a humidifier or cool-mist vaporizer. (If you don't have either of these fancy devices, an easy alternative is to take your baby into a steamy bathroom for about 15 minutes – you could even give her a nice warm bath at the same time!)

● **Try aromatherapy:** lavender, eucalyptus and Roman chamomile essential oils can all be used to ease congestion and aid your baby's breathing. Eucalyptus (diluted) can be used in nursery aromatherapy for symptomatic relief; its therapeutic effects can help to ease respiratory problems, including congestion, colds, flu and coughs. In addition to being a decongestant, it also has antiseptic and astringent properties that help to soothe mucus-membrane inflammation.

● **Use baby massage techniques on your baby's face,** as this can aid decongestion and help relieve painful sinuses (see pages 58–9).

● **Try reflexology** to stimulate your baby's sinuses and lungs, aiding the release of mucus and improving breathing (see page 69).

Fever

When your baby's body temperature rises above 37.5°C (100°F), this is referred to as a fever. It is not a disease or infection itself, but rather a symptom – a natural reaction of the human body when trying to tackle bacterial and viral infections.

This raising of bodily temperature is thought to be an attempt by your body to kill off the infection, although there are ongoing debates about the validity of this, and whether or not it is actually effective.

CAUSES AND SYMPTOMS

As mentioned above, fever is itself a symptom of something more serious, usually caused by bacteria or viruses, such as ear infections, flu, tonsillitis and a number of the common childhood illnesses. In addition to the raised temperature, which is best determined with a thermometer specifically designed for use with infants, the following symptoms often accompany a fever:

- Sweating
- Shivering
- Loss of appetite

NATURAL SOLUTIONS AND REMEDIES

Unless your baby's temperature is higher than those listed above, fevers do not normally need to be treated and may be allowed to run their course. However, there are a number of natural remedies that will help to reduce your baby's body temperature and ease her discomfort.

- **Bath your baby in lukewarm, not cold, water,** paying attention to how she reacts to the sudden change of temperature.
- **Dress your baby in lightweight clothes** to allow the extra body heat to escape from the skin.
- **Ensure your baby has plenty of fluids,** such as breast or formula milk, and water, if she's used to drinking it.
- **Try feeding garlic or lemon balm leaf,** as this may help – either in their food, for babies over five months old, or, if you're breastfeeding, take them yourself, as they will naturally pass on to your baby.
- **Try homeopathy:** Belladonna is recommended to help ease a fever (please seek advice from a trained homeopath before giving your child homeopathic remedies).

Cradle cap

While cradle cap doesn't look especially pleasant, it's actually a very common and completely harmless skin condition that affects the vast majority of young babies, though in rare cases it can last beyond the age of two. Despite its grisly appearance, babies and children rarely seem to suffer any itching or discomfort from it, even when accompanied by red patches on the forehead, and it's not in any way contagious.

CAUSES AND SYMPTOMS

The cause of cradle cap is not entirely obvious, but it is generally linked with oil-producing glands in the skin on a baby's head. When these become overactive for some reason, the result is the development of what look like yellowish, greasy scales that cover the scalp. As these scales begin to naturally flake and fall off, the hair sometimes comes away as well, though it soon grows back.

NATURAL SOLUTIONS AND REMEDIES

The temptation to pick off the scales as they begin to flake can be hard to resist, but resist it you must, as this can leave the skin underneath very raw and allow bacteria to get in and infect your baby's scalp. The scales will come off naturally and the cradle cap will clear up in its own time. However, there are a few things you can do to help it clear up more quickly.

- **Apply oil:** coconut oil, or olive oil mixed with a few drops of lavender oil, is an excellent, safe way to help the cradle cap loosen and fall off. Apply a small amount to the scalp, working it in gently, bearing in mind that babies' heads are quite soft. Using a fine-toothed comb, gently ease off those scales that come away without effort, but don't use any force or pick at them. Repeat each day until the scalp is clear.
- **Try homeopathy:** Calendula oil is recommended for daily use to help reduce the appearance of cradle cap.

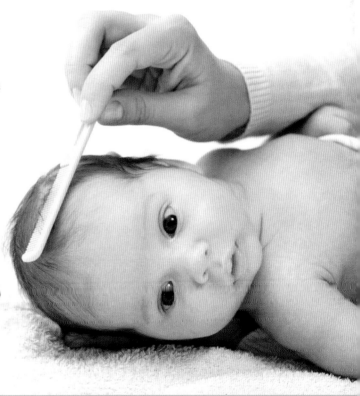

Eczema

One of the most common skin complaints, with up to 15 per cent of children in the UK affected, eczema can be a cause of concern for many parents. Put simply, eczema is an inflammation of the skin that causes itching and redness (often also referred to by doctors as dermatitis). There is no real 'cure' for eczema but, thankfully, there are plenty of ways to treat and prevent flare-ups safely and effectively.

CAUSES AND SYMPTOMS

The cause of eczema is unknown, but genes may be a factor: children are more likely to have it if a parent or close family member has had it too. Although it isn't an allergic reaction, eczema flare-ups can be caused by irritants in the air (such as pollen and cigarette smoke), or as a result of sensitivity to materials such as wool, for example, or to chemicals found in soaps or skin lotions. Some children may even develop eczema as a reaction to certain foodstuffs, although this is less common. In addition, stress can trigger an outbreak (this trigger may remain well into adulthood).

Eczema is generally always present in sufferers, in the form of dry skin. Flare-ups occur when the dry skin becomes inflamed (because the baby's immune system is fighting the problem) and present as a red, itchy, dry rash on the skin.

Eczema commonly occurs on the hands and feet, but can appear anywhere on the body.

NATURAL SOLUTIONS AND REMEDIES

Eczema can be so uncomfortable for little ones, but there are a number of things you can do to help to ease the itching and soreness often associated with the condition. Try some of the following:

● **Maintain a regular skin routine:** skin conditions such as eczema require regular treatment in order both to calm and prevent flare-ups. Regular baths are essential, as the water helps to soften the skin and loosen scabs; it also prepares the skin for moisturization. Make sure you use lukewarm water and a gentle bath wash – even natural ingredients can still be grown with chemicals that can irritate eczema, so always go for organic products if you can. If in doubt, avoid products containing chemicals such as SLS, parabens or petrochemicals, as these are known skin irritants.

● **Be kind to baby's skin.** After bathing, make sure you rinse your baby's skin thoroughly and pat it dry – don't rub with a towel, as this can irritate delicate skin.

● **Always moisturize!** This can help to soothe itching and prevent your little one from scratching, which in turn can cause secondary bacterial infections. It's important to moisturize within three minutes of your baby coming out of the bath, and always use oil rather than a lotion (again, make sure there are no harsh preservatives or ingredients, as mentioned above). Good ingredients to look for include vitamin E, helianthus oil, calendula oil and

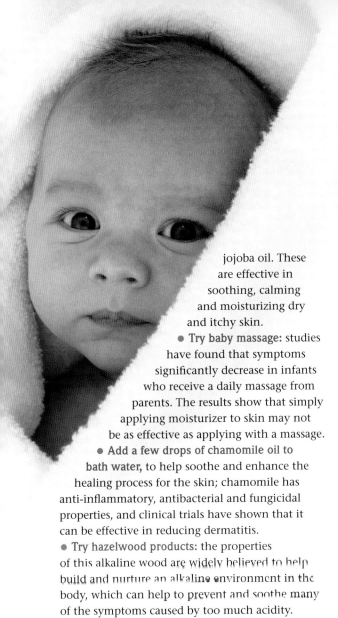

jojoba oil. These are effective in soothing, calming and moisturizing dry and itchy skin.

● **Try baby massage:** studies have found that symptoms significantly decrease in infants who receive a daily massage from parents. The results show that simply applying moisturizer to skin may not be as effective as applying with a massage.

● **Add a few drops of chamomile oil to bath water,** to help soothe and enhance the healing process for the skin; chamomile has anti-inflammatory, antibacterial and fungicidal properties, and clinical trials have shown that it can be effective in reducing dermatitis.

● **Try hazelwood products:** the properties of this alkaline wood are widely believed to help build and nurture an alkaline environment in the body, which can help to prevent and soothe many of the symptoms caused by too much acidity.

Wearing it as a necklace can help not only with eczema, but also with digestion, migraines, acid reflux, nausea, arthritis and other skin conditions.

● **Avoid processed foods,** if your baby is weaned – these often contain ingredients known to aggravate eczema. Instead, try to cook meals from scratch using locally sourced or organic ingredients.

● **Include probiotics and probiotic-rich foods in your baby's diet.** Much research has been done into how gut bacteria influences our health, and studies have shown that skin health is improved in patients who consume probiotics regularly.

● **Keep your baby hydrated:** water is essential for good health and even more so for eczema sufferers. Our bodies are made up of around 70 per cent water, which we lose throughout the day, so it's important to keep it topped up to help with skin hydration and overall health.

● **Dress your baby in organic clothing.** What your baby wears is just as important as what you put on their skin as an oil or lotion. Natural fibres such as cotton, organic cotton or silk are known to be much kinder to skin – unlike man-made fibres, which can cause discomfort and lead to scratching.

● **Wash your baby's clothes with care** – only use non-biological laundry products, or those made specifically for sensitive skin. Particles from laundry products are left in clothing after washing and react when we sweat, potentially causing reactions and irritations.

● **Make the bed kindly:** use anti-allergy bedding made from cotton or organic cotton, as this helps to keep dust mites at bay.

Nappy rash

This is another very common complaint

and, except in very severe cases, you don't need to consult your doctor. As the name suggests, nappy rash is a skin irritation on the baby's bottom or genital area – the parts usually covered by a nappy.

CAUSES AND SYMPTOMS

When your child's skin comes into continued contact with ammonia, which both urine and faeces contain, this can cause a pink or red rash in patches or spots. This is often sore and sensitive, and will cause your baby evident discomfort. Nappy rash can also be caused by fungal infections, which tend to develop in warm, humid conditions such as those found in nappies.

NATURAL SOLUTIONS AND REMEDIES

The best solution for nappy rash is prevention, which simply involves increasing the frequency with which you change your baby's nappy, and ensuring you change them as soon as possible after your baby has made use of them!

Unfortunately, it's not always possible to stop nappy rash developing, and the following can help to aid quick recovery:

● **Allow your baby as much time as possible without a nappy on,** as this will allow plenty of air to get to the affected areas. In case of accidents, it's worth lying your baby on a towel or, if she has

started rolling, crawling or is otherwise mobile, on a floor that is easy to wipe clean. Ensure the room is not too cold; you could even take her outside, if it's warm enough.

● **Try washing the affected area with a herbal infusion,** such as lavender or chamomile, which will help to protect your baby's skin and hasten the healing process.

● **Try homeopathy:** calendula cream is great for soothing the unpleasant burning and itching caused by nappy rash. Don't lay it on too thickly, though; apply a thin layer to the affected area (thin enough that you can clearly see the skin) before putting on a clean nappy. Calendula cream will also provide a layer that will protect your baby's skin from the effects of ammonia.

> **CAUTION**
>
> If the nappy rash has developed to the extent where the skin is cracked or broken, or blisters or swellings have appeared, take your baby to the doctor, as this may be a sign that there is some kind of infection.

Constipation

Simply put, constipation is when faeces becomes harder and drier than usual, making it difficult and even painful to go to the toilet.

If your infant is suffering from this condition, this may be indicated by evident discomfort when she is trying to empty her bowels, or she may not go to the toilet as often as she usually does.

CAUSES

Most of us will be familiar with this unpleasant condition, which can have a variety of causes – the majority of which are not serious. If constipation is not dealt with quickly, however, it can result in problems due to the build-up of waste product in your baby's intestines.

The following are the most common causes:
- Dehydration, especially in hot weather, as it causes faeces to dry out more quickly than usual
- Certain types of food, since constipation is concerned with the digestive system:
  - a diet that is too low in fibre or too high in dairy products
  - other starchy or stodgy foods, such as bread, pasta, cereal, potatoes and bananas

Bottle-fed babies often suffer in this way because formula milk is much harder to digest than breast milk (breast milk is easier for a child to digest than pretty much anything else, so when you start to wean your breastfed baby onto solid food, you may find she suffers from constipation).

NATURAL SOLUTIONS AND REMEDIES

While simply changing your baby's diet will often relieve constipation, there are other treatments you can try that may also help to get things softened up and on the move:

- **Try fruit juices:** some juices, such as grape and prune juice, can help relieve constipation, though it's a good idea to talk to your healthcare provider before introducing new foods to very young babies. Around 50 ml (2 fl oz) of diluted fruit juice twice a day is usually recommended.
- **Give your baby (if weaned) high-fibre foods,** such as fruit (not bananas), vegetables, beans and wholemeal grain foods; these will help tackle constipation. Avoid giving too much squash or milk, which tends to have the opposite effect.

- Try alternating the following two exercises:
- Gently massage and rub your baby's tummy in a spiral motion, starting at the belly button and gradually moving outwards. As the digestive tract is laid out in a clockwise direction, it's important not to massage anti-clockwise.
- With your baby lying on her back with her legs lightly held in a half-bent position, slowly move the legs as though pedalling a bicycle. This can also help to relieve excess gas.
- **Bath your baby in warm water with a drop of lavender essential oil.** This has two benefits, as the lavender will help ease any pain caused by the constipation, while the warmth of the water should help to relax your baby, allowing 'things' to get

moving. While drying your baby, it may help to give her a gentle tummy massage as well (see pages 50–52).
- **Try reflexology** – this will help with relaxation, and the reflex points can also work on the digestive tract, combating constipation (see page 68).
- **Try homeopathy:** Bryonia (bryony) is helpful for relieving dehydration and general dryness, and so is recommended for constipation. Nux Vomica can also assist when your baby clearly wants to go to the loo though without success. (Please seek advice from a quailfied homeopath before giving homeopathic remedies to your baby.)

Diarrhoea

Essentially the opposite of constipation, diarrhoea is often more concerning and distressing, though neither condition is pleasant. It is usually defined as the passing of loose or watery faeces at least six times in a single day – often at the most inconvenient of times for parents to deal with!

CAUSES

There are a number of things that can cause babies to suffer from diarrhoea, including bacterial or viral infections, intolerance to certain types of food that they find hard to digest, teething, or it may be that something has upset your baby or made her anxious.

The bottom line is that, while with constipation too much fluid is absorbed from the bowel, with diarrhoea something is preventing that fluid from being absorbed properly.

NATURAL SOLUTIONS AND REMEDIES

When your baby is suffering from diarrhoea it's very important to bear in mind the risk of dehydration, as she will

be losing a lot of valuable fluid. Make sure you keep her topped up with plenty of cooled boiled water or extra milk, to maintain healthy fluid levels. In addition to this, try the following to help tackle this unpleasant ailment:

● **Feed weaned babies mashed ripe banana** – this will help their digestive system recover. Adding a teaspoonful of pectin-rich carob powder will also assist in binding things together.

● **Give your baby some aniseed water,** as this will help to calm upset intestines and encourage gas to be passed. Simply grind one or two points of star anise as finely as possible and pour half a cup of boiling water over it. Once this has cooled, use a dropper to give your baby 3–6 drops orally whenever there are signs of an upset stomach.

Gastro-oesophageal reflux (GOR)

If your baby starts to burp before bringing up a small amount of milk (also known as posseting), the chances are she is suffering from a common complaint known as reflux.

Up to 70 per cent of three- to seven-month-old babies will bring up the contents of their stomach more than once a day. This is due to milk-based foods combining with the child's stomach acid, causing a reaction that pushes the acid into the oesophagus, as an undeveloped muscular valve means that the baby can't fully keep the regurgitation down.

SYMPTOMS

- A disinclination to gain, or reduction in, weight
- Inconsolability, as a result of stomach pain
- Grumpiness during or after feed
- Fatigue
- Regurgitation
- Inability to settle for long periods of time
- Coughing
- Arching away when feeding, or refusing to feed

A variation on this condition, known as silent reflux (laryngopharyngeal reflux/LPR), has no outward symptoms, which can make it difficult to identify. However, if your child shows

CAUTION

Reflux is a common infant complaint, particularly during the first three months, but if symptoms persist or you have any cause for concern check with your doctor, especially if any of the following symptoms are present:
- Severe constipation
- Bloody or completely black stools
- Choking or blue colouring in the face
- Continuous refusal of food
- Fever
- Renewed bouts of vomiting after six months
- Stomach distension
- Bile (green vomit)
- Projectile vomiting

discomfort, irritability or pain when lying down, or a persistent, chronic cough, then she may be experiencing this intestinal complaint. Similarly, LPR is characterized by a sore throat, hoarse cry and persistent cough, with the throat and nasal passage exhibiting tenderness due to the stomach acid.

NATURAL SOLUTIONS AND REMEDIES

Treating this complaint can be as simple as watching what you eat and changing the way you feed your child, but there are other remedies that can help, too. Natural remedies worked well to ease my own daughter's symptoms; ultimately, it was a relief to be able to alleviate her pain without having to rely on needless medication.

• **Monitor your diet if breastfeeding.** Some babies experience a worsening of symptoms because their tiny digestive systems can't tolerate certain foods, so cut out common irritants to see if it helps: these include dairy, soya, eggs, peanuts, gluten, caffeine and spicy foods. Cut out several foods at once, then add them back in one at a time and see if any of them bother your baby. Try eliminating excess carbs, too: studies have found that putting reflux sufferers on a low-carb diet is a reliable treatment for reflux, as the oesophageal sphincter is controlled by insulin. It thus follows that sugar is a main dietary culprit in a child who suffers from reflux.

• **Try drinking chamomile tea** if you're breastfeeding, as this can help to soothe pain and relieve stomach discomfort when passed through your milk.

• **Elevate your baby's head while eating.** Put a pillow under her head so that, as she eats, the milk goes down into her belly instead of staying up in her oesophagus. Try to keep her upright after feeds and at other times, such as nappy changes and bathtime, too.

• **Feed little and often:** symptoms can be made worse when your baby drinks too much milk in one go, so smaller feeds more often may help. If you're breastfeeding and have forceful let-down, make sure to nurse in positions that allow your baby better control of how much milk she's getting. Remember to burp your baby after every feed and keep her upright while you do this.

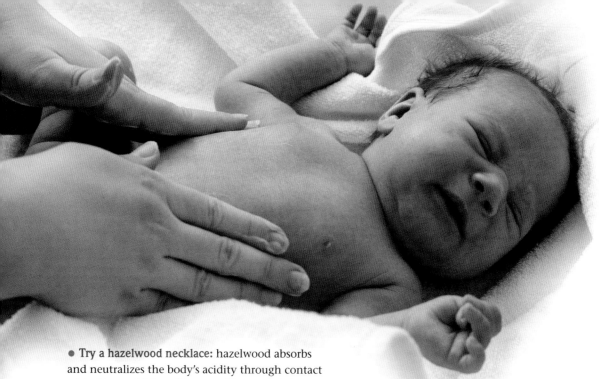

- **Try a hazelwood necklace:** hazelwood absorbs and neutralizes the body's acidity through contact with skin, and I found it very effective at helping to ease the acidity related to my children's reflux.
- **Wear your baby!** Babies love to be worn, and a carrier that allows your baby to be more upright, with no pressure on the belly, should reduce the likelihood of a reflux episode.
- **Try chiropractic care:** some babies may have reflux because they simply are out of alignment due to the birth process. If you do choose to take your baby to a chiropractor, make sure they are very experienced with babies and also that they do very light adjustments (when adjusting your baby, it should look like a light massage).
- **Try baby massage:** this can help improve a slow and immature digestive system by toning the digestive tract and maturing the entire system. All you need is some organic baby oil to soothe your little one's tummy – add a drop of lavender or chamomile to 30 ml (1 fl oz) of oil to help comfort and calm your baby.
- **Try homeopathy:** a proven remedy for reflux is Nat Phos 6x – dose 1 tablet dissolved in milk given immediately after a feed. Alternatively, if you're breastfeeding, take Nat Phos 6x – dose 2 tablets after each meal, three times a day; your milk will pass the effect to your baby, gently and naturally. (Please seek the advice of a trained homeopath before giving a homeopathic remedy to your infant.)

Teething

You will no doubt find that the moment your baby starts making any kind of fuss or looking slightly pink around the cheeks everyone assumes teething is the problem, and will happily start advising you on various methods to tackle the issue.

Unsurprisingly, these affable assumptions, and accompanying barrage of advice, are not always a great help – not every whinge or yawn is an indication of teething, and nor is every treatment necessarily suitable.

Thankfully, there are some key symptoms to help spot teething, together with a number of simple, natural therapies that can soothe your baby's discomfort at this time.

CAUSES AND SYMPTOMS

As the name suggests, 'teething' is simply the process of a child's teeth growing through the gum, which begins around the age of six months. While teething is a perfectly normal and natural part of your baby's development, it can nonetheless be a distressing time for both of you, as many babies find teething painful, or at least a discomfort.

Although it's not always easy to tell if your baby is teething, the usual symptoms associated with it include:

- Red cheeks that feel hot to the touch
- Diarrhoea, often with accompanying nappy rash
- Disturbed sleep patterns, including a difficulty getting to sleep
- A desire to chew on objects even more than usual
- An excessive amount of dribbling compared to usual

NATURAL SOLUTIONS AND REMEDIES

You will inevitably find yourself inundated with advice on how to tackle your baby's teething, but here are a number of tried-and-tested solutions and remedies – see which ones work for you and your baby:

● **Offer your baby a clean finger to chew on.** This is one of the best and oldest methods of easing the discomfort of teething – the pressure of champing away at your finger helps relieve the pressure of the tooth pushing its way through the gum. Not only that, but this is also good bonding time for baby and parents.

● **Give your baby frozen items to chew on** (as an alternative to your finger), including:

● breast milk, water or diluted chamomile tea placed in ice-cube trays and left to go solid in the freezer. Don't give your baby the cubes whole, but crush them up first by placing them in a sterilized cloth and giving them a bash with a pan or rolling pin. Your baby can then chew on these frozen chips.

● fruit: freeze it and place it in a mesh feeder (available from childcare stores or online). Banana is especially beneficial, as it also helps to reduce diarrhoea, which is a common side effect of teething.

● pieces of cloth placed in the freezer for a couple of hours, dipped first in either water or chamomile tea (which has the added bonus of helping to soothe and relax your baby).

● **Try massaging your baby's face around the gum area:** this can not only help relieve teething pain, but can also ease ear- and headaches that are often caused by teething (see page 59).

● **Give your baby an amber teething necklace:** amber is a natural painkiller and a great alternative to over-the-counter pain relief; when worn on the skin, it releases healing oils that help your baby to stay calm and more relaxed throughout the teething period.

● **Try drinking chamomile tea or taking flower remedies,** if you are breastfeeding your baby, as these will then be passed on to your infant and can help to soothe their teething pains.

● **Apply rescue remedy or other suitable flower remedies to your baby's gums** – simply dilute them in cooled boiled water and rub them gently onto the gums to soothe the pain.

● **Try homeopathy:** Chamomilla is recommended for babies who become irritable and make a fuss while teething, while Pulsatilla is suggested if your baby becomes clingy. (Always seek the advice of a trained homeopath before giving a homeopathic remedy to your infant.)

Sleep deprivation

As the name suggests, sleep deprivation is the result of your baby not getting sufficient sleep. This often results in the infant becoming overtired, and so finding it harder to settle to sleep, and the longer it takes her to get to sleep, the further away that blissful state appears.

As a parent, this vicious cycle can be very frustrating, so to help in getting your baby to sleep, it's useful to understand how certain hormones affect sleep and can end up causing sleep deprivation.

CAUSES AND SYMPTOMS

Cortisol (the stress hormone) is one of the hormones that govern the sleep/wake cycle; another is melatonin, which helps to regulate our body clock. The level of these two hormones changes during the day, with cortisol peaking in the morning, and so keeping us awake, and melatonin increasing as the light fades, thus helping us to prepare for sleep (and making us tired for most of the winter!). If you work together with these hormones, it will be that much easier to get your baby to sleep – encouraging the brain to release melatonin while restricting the production of cortisol.

Sleep deprivation is caused by allowing your baby to become overtired, or stimulating them when it's time for them to sleep, because these both force the brain to release cortisol in an attempt to keep the baby alert. While sleep deprivation is not easy to spot, the infant will give off cues that they are tired, such as rubbing their eyes, yawning or trying to turn away from anything that is exciting or stimulating. These are usually followed by attempts at self-soothing, such as thumb-sucking, crying for a dummy or rocking the head.

NATURAL SOLUTIONS AND REMEDIES

The best method to counter overtiredness is to try and ensure your baby has a good routine that involves her being settled down to sleep at suitable times, with only short awake times in between (45 minutes for newborns, up to four hours for six-month-olds, and between four and five hours for toddlers). After this awake time, your baby will become sleepy, and if you settle her quickly you will find that the melatonin kicks in, outweighing the diminishing effects of

cortisol, and causing her to fall asleep easily.

Despite your best efforts, however, there will be times when – for one reason or another – your baby ends up being deprived of sleep, and so the battle to get her to sleep begins! There are probably as many suggestions for getting babies to sleep as there are nursing mothers, or at least as many as there are opinionated grandmothers! But at the core of any sleep-inducing strategy is the need for sensory soothing that will help to settle your baby. This is especially true of babies whose overtiredness has led to a cycle of crying.

The following tactics have been tried and tested for many years:

● **Hold your baby close to your body** in a firm, comforting grip (use your forearms as well as your hands).
● **Swaddle your baby** in such a way that her arms and legs are held firmly, but gently, in place (see page 23 for swaddling instructions).
● **Rock your baby,** simply in your arms.
● **Take your baby into a dark room** to cut down on visual stimulation.
● **Feed your baby** so that she settles down but doesn't actually fall asleep.
● **Make use of nursery aromatherapy or play white noise** (available free on the internet) to help soothe and settle your baby (see pages 21–2 for aromatherapy advice).
● **Use the 5-minute bedtime-massage routine** to help reduce levels of cortisol and increase the production of the relaxing 'trust hormone', oxytocin (see pages 62–5).

Happy mum equals
happy baby
chapter seven

The arrival of a new baby will of course supply a limitless amount of joy. But becoming a mother is one of the biggest changes a woman will ever face, and it's completely normal that the transition to the world of motherhood will bring its own challenges. New mothers respond in their own unique way to the changes in their postnatal life, body and emotional state; while some may slot straight into their new role without issue, others may find it overwhelming and confusing.

As babies are incredibly perceptive when it comes to their mother's moods, the contentment of a new family is co-dependent: a happy mum equals a happy child – and vice versa. It's natural to experience a certain amount of stress, but if this anxiety begins to escalate, it can have an impact on the care and attention a mother is able to provide for her newborn. This, in turn, can result in the child feeling insecure and isolated; research has shown that a child's physical and mental development is strongly linked to feelings of security and emotional well-being. It has also been found that the longer the child's needs go unaddressed, the longer the detrimental effects will last sometimes even into adulthood.

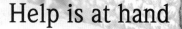

Help is at hand

The good news is that help can be found in a variety of forms. The postnatal period can extend for months, so it's important for new mothers to be able to draw on the support of others during this time.

Encouragement derived from the kind words of others will allow you to gain confidence while assisting your recovery. It will also help to reassure you that any small oversights made during your daily life are normal, and that your best efforts are being celebrated.

Breastfeeding helps to strengthen the bond between mother and child, and – crucially – may also provide protection against postpartum illness; recent research has found that the feel-good hormones oxytocin and prolactin, released during breastfeeding, lower stress levels while allowing the new mother to feel calmer in challenging situations. This may have a positive impact on mental health, decreasing the symptoms of postpartum depression and allowing you to feel more in control.

Holistic therapies are also an excellent way of balancing out hormone levels and promoting sleep and relaxation. They have even been known to deliver organic pain relief and strengthen the immune system – all without the aid of manufactured and potentially harmful chemicals. Mums who are more relaxed are better at coping with the pressures of family life – and with a greater sense of well-being that will be passed on to the baby. As these remedies are natural, they are also safe to use in their prescribed quantities while nursing your child (though do seek the advice of a medical professional if you are ever unsure).

The following pages offer an overview of recommended therapies and how they can help, then in chapter 8 you will find more specific advice on how to use these therapies to alleviate a range of common ailments.

Recommended holistic therapies

Nothing throws a household into chaos like the arrival of a new baby. However, it's important to remember that **your** needs must be addressed, as well as those of your child's. The physical and emotional exertions of childbirth can be well countered in a range of different ways.

EXERCISE

Getting back into shape after childbirth is a concern for many women. The effects of giving birth will permeate your physical self deeply, but light exercise and toning will ensure that you begin to recognize your pre-pregnancy body. Key areas that should be strengthened as soon as possible are the pelvic floor, back and stomach muscles, once approval has been given by your care-provider.

HOMEOPATHY

Homeopathy's holistic approach towards medicine means that it encourages the body to heal itself. Non-toxic, and with an excellent safety track record, this natural treatment is particularly useful following labour, and can help you recover from loss of blood and hormonal imbalances. Homeopathic treatments also work well to address the common ailments a child faces within the first year of life, such as colic, cradle cap, constipation and teething (see chapter 6).

TRY YOGA

Yoga classes are a great way of toning up while allowing you to bask in the deep relaxation the exercise provides. Yoga's ability to supply relief to the shoulder and neck areas particularly affected by carrying a child, along with breathing techniques designed to lower anxiety, will also be a benefit for the months – even years – to come.

POSTPARTUM MASSAGE

Massage therapy is one of the most beneficial therapies new mothers can undertake. Its ability to relax ensures that the task of motherhood will be met with a clearer head; after all, a mother who feels looked after herself is better able to look after her child. Not only does the practice promote feelings of well-being and emotional calm, it also has a wide range of physiological benefits. From draining excess fluids within the tissues and toning the abdominal muscles, to realigning the spine and pelvic structures, postpartum massage can speed up the process of your physical recovery in the most relaxing way possible.

FLOWER ESSENCES

Part of a progressive new field of alternative treatment, flower essences provide inner balance by using only the natural energies of plants. Designed to settle and soothe anxieties, they can help you to cope with pregnancy, labour and the relationship with your child after the birth. They come in the form of distilled plant preparations and use the key characteristics of the flower as a remedy for an emotional ailment.

AROMATHERAPY

From the smell of baked bread to a lightly fragranced breeze, our sense of smell has long been known to trigger emotional responses – including the resurgence of memories from long-forgotten moments. This is because our sense of smell has its roots in the limbic system – the area of the

SCENT SENSE

Integrating an aromatherapy routine into your life will allow you some time to counter the stresses and strains of motherhood, simply by enabling you time away to address your own needs, in your own space.

brain also responsible for memory, as well as for the stimulation of the hypothalamus and pituitary glands. When these two areas are triggered, they can release positive hormones, which is why aromatherapy is particularly useful for enhancing feelings of well-being and calm.

Whether you choose to disperse the scent of aromatherapy oils around the home, use them in combination with a relaxing massage, or add a few drops to your bath water, the therapeutic benefits of their natural fragrances cannot be disputed.

REFLEXOLOGY

From birth, our sense of touch is the most highly developed sense that we possess. Reflexology draws on this, as well as the relationship between pressure points in the hands and feet to other areas of the body, to promote a sense of harmony and relaxation. Stimulation of these areas ensures that energy is free to flow throughout the body, and that the body's natural pre-pregnancy balance is restored.

SELF-CARE

Although many parents claim that sleep is a thing that escapes them on a nightly basis, there is nothing more important when it comes to your physical recovery and spiritual rejuvenation. Emotional and physical stress will only be increased when attempting to provide care for an infant while depleted of energy. Traditionally, new mothers are advised that trivial matters such as housework, cooking and entertaining should be shelved during recovery – and this is advice that should be heeded. Minimize any extra exertions, and always attempt to sleep when your child is sleeping, especially during the first six weeks after the birth.

Of equal importance is ensuring that you're eating the right foods on your road to recovery. Eat healthily, making sure you're taking in extra vitamins, minerals and iron-rich foods, especially if you are breastfeeding. Keep hydration levels topped up at all times by drinking water regularly or enjoying herbal teas, which have the added benefit of enhancing a sense of well-being. Nuts, seeds and meat, as well as plenty of fresh fruit and vegetables, are essential foods that should be on every new mother's shopping list.

Common ailments
in new mums
chapter eight

If you're a new mum, then it's likely you'll experience at least one or more of the following conditions. But don't despair – there are plenty of natural solutions and remedies you can try at home to alleviate your symptoms.

Postnatal depression

As the name suggests, postnatal (or postpartum) depression is a form of depression which occurs after giving birth. Around one in six mothers suffers from this condition, although it's not always diagnosed, let alone treated.

No one is entirely sure exactly what causes postnatal depression, and it could well be that a number of different factors play a part. Physiologically, after giving birth there is a sudden drop in hormones such as oestrogen and progesterone, which can cause a depression-inducing chemical imbalance in the brain. Psychologically, if you have suffered from, for want of a better word, 'normal' depression in the past, this may make you more likely to suffer from postnatal depression, too. Socially, after the excitement of the baby's arrival and the stream of visitors starts to ebb, this can leave the new mums feeling somewhat lost and alone.

While it is normal to suffer mood swings – known as 'baby blues' – during the first few weeks after birth, it could be a sign of postnatal depression if these symptoms don't clear up

SIGNS OF POSTNATAL DEPRESSION INCLUDE:

- Feeling very low, or despondent, thinking that nothing is any good, or that life is a long, grey tunnel without end or hope

- Feeling tired and lethargic, or sometimes feeling numb, not wanting to do anything or take an interest in the outside world

- A sense of inadequacy – of feeling unable to cope

- Feeling guilty about not coping or about not loving your baby enough

- Being unusually irritable, which has the unfortunate tendency of making the guilt worse

- Being tearful and crying, or at least wanting to cry

- Losing your appetite, which may go with feeling hungry all the time but simply being unable to eat

- Difficulty sleeping – either not getting to sleep or waking early, or having vivid nightmares

- Being hostile or indifferent to your husband or partner

- Being hostile or indifferent to your baby

- Loss of libido

- Having panic attacks, which strike at any time, causing rapid heartbeat, sweaty palms and feelings of sickness or faintness

- An overpowering anxiety, often about things that wouldn't normally bother you, such as being alone in the house

- Difficulty in concentrating or making decisions

- Physical symptoms, such as stomach pains, headaches and blurred vision

- Obsessive fears about your baby's health or well-being, or about yourself and other members of the family

within a month. Postnatal depression usually develops within the first six weeks after giving birth, but it's not restricted to this time-frame and there are many cases where it doesn't fully set in for a number of months. Partners and others close to the new mother need to keep an eye out for the symptoms, so it can be diagnosed and dealt with as swiftly as possible. And, if you are suffering from postnatal depression yourself, it's important to bear in mind that it is an illness, so try not to feel guilty about how you may feel towards your new baby.

Complementary therapies are well worth looking into if you feel you are suffering from any of the symptoms listed opposite; many women find herbal remedies and homeopathy especially helpful. In adition, massage, reflexology and aromatherapy can be a natural self-healing tool for postnatal depression. You should also look at your nutrition, to help rebalance your hormones and so regain your energy levels.

It's important to feel understood and supported throughout this huge transitional stage in your life. A sympathetic listener, who allows you to express your feelings and worries without fear of judgement, can bring enormous relief. It could be your health visitor or partner, a community psychiatric nurse, a counsellor or simply a friend. Don't suffer in silence; after all, a problem shared is a problem halved.

NATURAL SOLUTIONS AND REMEDIES
▶▶ AROMATHERAPY
Try and take some time out for yourself each day. Ask your partner or someone close to you to take over, even if it's just for fifteen or twenty minutes. Fight the urge to feel guilty asking for this time – remember that your partner needs time to form a close bond with the baby, too. During this break, try and relax; having a nice warm soak in the bath is a great way to accomplish this. Add 4 to 6 drops of rose otto or jasmine oil to your bath to help ease symptoms of postnatal depression; jasmine and rose are 'feminine' oils that help balance hormones, promote relaxation and release oxytocin in your body.

The table below lists a selection of other oils that can be helpful during the postnatal period. These are feminine oils that will make you feel special, calm you down, strengthen the nervous system and, in their own unique way, help lift depression.

OILS TO LIFT DEPRESSION	POSITIVE ATTRIBUTES
Bergamot	Good for emotional imbalances and burn-out caused by sleep deprivation, aiding motivation and creating confidence.
Clary sage	Good for nervousness, stress and emotional debility. Aids in grounding and rebalancing the body's systems.
Grapefruit	Helps with sadness and self-criticism, instead promoting a feeling of joyfulness. A very positive oil.
Mandarin	Eases the feelings of emptiness that depression can bring, calming the nervous system and leaving the body relaxed.
Geranium	Helps with extreme mood swings, insecurity and over-sensitivity. Geranium is a 'mothering' oil to the new mother herself.
Jasmine	A very soothing oil – excellent for easing feelings of depression and low self-esteem. Jasmine can help with guilt, anxiety and tension.
Neroli	Neroli can help with the shock of going through a Caesarean birth. It also lifts melancholy and panic, making it very beneficial for dealing with depression.

HOMEOPATHY

Homeopathic remedies are great for helping mothers emotionally after giving birth, when many women feel low and may become withdrawn and tearful. To ease the feelings of postnatal depression, homeopaths suggest taking Arnica 6c to help stabilize hormones and emotions, and St John's Wort to alleviate depression.

HERBAL REMEDIES

Drink teas such as lemon balm, peppermint or orange blossom to lift your mood, promoting happiness and well-being. You can also take a daily supplement of St John's Wort to help rebalance your hormones and lift the dark feelings that accompany depression.

REFLEXOLOGY

The effects of reflexology can be helpful during the postnatal period to rebalance the hormonal and digestive systems, which get knocked out of balance during pregnancy and birth. Reflexology with a qualified practitioner will help bring your body back into harmony, creating feelings of health and well-being. It can also be very beneficial psychologically, as it will help you unwind and give you the opportunity to talk freely in a relaxing environment, if you feel the need.

FLOWER REMEDIES

Most flower remedies offer benefits that can help with postnatal depression; those most commonly used to counter this condition are listed above.

FLOWER REMEDIES	BENEFITS
Crab apple	Eases trauma and feelings of self-loathing and even self-disgust.
Elm	Helps if you are feeling overwhelmed by the responsibilities of being a new parent.
Pine	If you need to regain perspective, pine can help with the shock of birth (especially an emergency C-section) and feelings of failure.
Red chestnut	Targets feelings of anxiety that are common in postnatal depression.
Mustard	Helps you to cope if you're feeling very low and depressed but aren't really sure why.

NUTRITION

Take a zinc supplement and vitamin B to rebalance the hormones after birth.

Breastfeeding problems

Breast milk is always the best food for your baby, and the benefits of breastfeeding extend well beyond basic nutrition. However, breastfeeding is not always as easy, nor does it necessarily feel as natural, as you may have anticipated.

If you can persevere with it you will reap the benefits, due to its supply of all the vitamins and nutrients your baby needs in the first six months of life. Breast milk is packed with disease-fighting substances, such as antibodies that build up your baby's immune system and protect your baby from illness.

COMMON COMPLAINTS

▶▶ AN UNSETTLED BABY

If your baby is unsettled at the breast and also unsettled after a feed, it may be that he's not attached correctly, limiting his milk supply. Ask your health visitor about local breastfeeding groups that can teach you good positioning to aid better attachment, so your baby can get a good feed. (See page 124 for information on finding a breastfeeding group or supporter in your area.)

▶▶ SORE OR CRACKED NIPPLES

If your nipples hurt, remove your baby from your breast and try again. To do this, slide a finger gently into the corner of your baby's mouth until his tongue releases. Don't put up with the pain; pain usually results from incorrect attachment that will not allow your baby to feed properly. If, even after reattaching, the pain continues, or if your nipples start to crack or bleed, ask a breastfeeding supporter to show you how to attach your baby correctly. Pain is not normal, so do ask for help and support.

➤➤ SORE BREASTS, BLOCKED DUCTS AND MASTITIS

It's important to deal with a sore breast or a blocked duct as soon as possible by seeking professional help, so that it doesn't lead to mastitis (inflammation of the breast). If you do develop mastitis, you're likely to have at least two of the following symptoms:

- Breasts that feel hot and tender
- A red patch of skin that is painful to touch
- General feeling of illness, as if you have the flu
- Feeling achy, tired and tearful
- An increased temperature

This can happen very suddenly and can quickly get worse. It is important to carry on breastfeeding, as this helps to speed up your recovery.

➤➤ INSUFFICIENT MILK SUPPLY

Unlike drink bottles for babies, breasts don't come with a handy guide showing the amount of milk they contain! As such, it can be all too easy for a nursing mother to become concerned about the sufficiency of her milk supply, and worries over this issue are the most common cause for mothers switching to formula milk or weaning their babies early.

DID YOU KNOW?

Raw, cooled cabbage leaves can be used to soothe engorged breasts: apply clean, chilled inner leaves as a compress, changing them every two hours or so, or when the leaves wilt.

It's true that some mothers, no matter what they try, simply don't produce enough milk, but the actual percentage of those with a genuinely insufficient supply is very low indeed. Lower still are those who produce no milk at all, and, unless you're in this small minority, you should be able to keep producing milk for your baby for as long as necessary, though supplementing with formula milk may be required.

NATURAL SOLUTIONS AND REMEDIES FOR MASTITIS

Try these general tips, in addition to the specific remedies outlined overleaf:

- Check and improve the attachment of your baby at the breast (ask your midwife, health visitor or

> ### PREVENTATIVE PREPARATION
>
> Olive oil, sweet almond oil, lanolin or comfrey ointment rubbed into the nipples throughout the latter part of the pregnancy and the early weeks of nursing creates healthy, flexible tissues that are very resistant to cracks, tears and chapping.

volunteer breastfeeding supporter).

● **Express some milk by hand to relieve the fullness,** if your breasts still feel full after a feed or your baby cannot feed.

● **Warm your breasts before a feed,** as this can help the milk to flow and make you feel more comfortable. Try warm flannels or have a bath or shower.

● **Gently stroke the lumpy or tender area towards your nipple with your fingertips,** while your baby is feeding. This should help the milk to flow from these areas.

● **Get as much rest as possible.**

▶▶ AROMATHERAPY

Relieve some of the discomfort of mastitis and ease swelling by soaking in a bath containing 4 drops of geranium oil and 1 drop of Roman chamomile oil. Always apply the appropriate essential oils immediately after each feed, so that they are completely absorbed by your body before your baby's next feed is due.

▶▶ HOMEOPATHY

If one (or both) of your breasts becomes red, inflamed and itchy, try Bryonia 30c. If they are hot, swollen and you have a fever, try Belladonna 30c.

▶▶ HERBAL REMEDIES

If you're suffering with a fever, try drinking elderflower tea to relieve the discomfort.

NATURAL SOLUTIONS AND REMEDIES FOR SORE AND CRACKED NIPPLES

▶▶ HOMEOPATHY

For sore and cracked nipples that are bleeding and swollen, try Graphite 6c. For red, stinging and burning nipples, try Staphysagria 6c. If the pain in your nipples is accompanied by tearfulness, try Pulsatilla 6c.

▶▶ HERBAL REMEDIES

Yarrow leaf or yarrow-infused oil can provide almost instantaneous pain relief and heal cracked nipples rapidly. The gel from a fresh aloe vera leaf will soothe and heal sore and cracked nipples, and calendula ointment is an old favourite for healing and strengthening nipples.

▶▶ NATURAL CARE

Avoid wearing a bra 24 hours a day. Wear nursing bras with the flaps down whenever possible. Expose your nipples and breasts to the air as much as you can to discourage the growth of infection or risk of thrush. Also expose them to sunlight for brief periods to strengthen tissues, if possible,

increasing gradually from 30 seconds in the sun to a maximum of 3 minutes.

NATURAL SOLUTIONS AND REMEDIES FOR AN INSUFFICIENT MILK SUPPLY

▶ MASSAGE
Massaging your baby enhances the secretion of prolactin, essential for milk production, so easing the process of breastfeeding.

▶ AROMATHERAPY
Fennel oil encourages milk production. Fennel will also help to keep the baby's stools normal and can help to relieve wind. Alternatively, you can drink fennel tea to aid in milk production.

If you have the opposite problem, in that you produce too much milk, you can balance the production of your milk supply by adding 2 drops of peppermint oil to 4 drops of geranium oil and massaging the oil all over your breasts.

Hormone imbalance

As mentioned earlier, levels of hormones such as oestrogen and progesterone tend to be all over the place after giving birth. When you then add to this the stresses of living with a new baby – poor sleep, coping with breastfeeding, nappy changing, adjustments to family life, and so on – it's no wonder you can end up feeling worn out and irritable.

Unfortunately, this tends to upset hormone levels even further, as your body attempts to cope with the stress and keep you functioning through the sleep-deprived fog and emotional instability. This is when your adrenal glands kick in, working overtime to pump another hormone – adrenaline – into your system, giving you the boost you need to keep going. Sadly, this extra hormonal energy comes at a price, and can leave you feeling even more tired, irritable and emotional than you were before.

Cortisol levels may also get knocked out of balance at this time; cortisol tries to come to the rescue by releasing more energy into your system through the conversion of proteins. While cortisol can do a good job at countering the effects of an adrenaline overload, if it is not stopped it will, in turn, put other hormones out of balance. As you can see, being a new mum can have a major effect on your hormones; it's hardly surprising that emotions can be a little up and down!

Thankfully, there are a number of natural solutions and remedies that can help to correct these hormone imbalances, calming the emotional rollercoaster and so leaving you better able to cope and look forward to life with your new baby.

Many chronic illnesses in new mums go untreated because symptoms are mistaken for common complaints of sleep-deprived parents. 'Well, you just had a baby' can answer for a lot of problems, but sometimes there's more to the story. Some women suffer more intense, longer-lasting postnatal troubles that can threaten their health – and these troubles may be directly related to hormone imbalance. Looking after your health and your body during this period will ensure that you thrive as a mother.

NATURAL SOLUTIONS AND REMEDIES

REFLEXOLOGY

Reflexology is excellent for rebalancing the body after childbirth. Women experience many postnatal symptoms as the hormone levels in the body – and the body itself – readjust after the months of pregnancy. As the hormonal system is very easily upset by such factors as stress, sleep deprivation and tension, it's no wonder that it can take the body's system a while to rebalance itself in the postnatal period. Working the reflex of the pituary gland (the 'master gland') helps the hormonal levels to regain balance, and leaves the new mother feeling more relaxed.

AROMATHERAPY

There are a number of oils that can help with hormone imbalance:

OILS FOR HORMONE IMBALANCE	POSITIVE ATTRIBUTES
Peppermint	Helps with mental fatigue, feelings of helplessness and being overworked.
Ylang ylang	Good for easing irritability, resentment and emotional guilt.
Frankincense	Helps with over-attachment issues, anxiety and fear.
Rose	The most beneficial oil for rebalancing and soothing the nervous system, leaving a sense of inner vitality and calm.

►► MASSAGE

In the midst of all the hormonal changes and emotional ups and downs, massage can help to provide some much needed soothing, relaxation and easing of physical discomfort. Remember that many of the hormones pumping around your system are busy undoing the physical changes that have occurred in the last nine and a half months. Your uterus, breasts, pelvic floor and abdominal muscles are all going through these adjustments, which can lead to severe cramps and general aching.

As such, regular massage during the first months after giving birth can be very beneficial, tackling both the physical and emotional stresses of this time. Performed correctly, postnatal massage can reduce the effects of stress hormones, such as adrenaline and cortisol, encourage lactation, relieve muscular cramps and soreness, and generally encourage an improved emotional state.

GIVE AND RECEIVE

In addition to receiving massage yourself, massaging your newborn baby can help to relieve some of the stresses and emotions of early motherhood. This helps both recipient and masseuse to relax, at the same time strengthening the bond between you.

Caesarean section

Whether planned or carried out as an emergency procedure, Caesarean section (or C-section) deliveries can often leave mothers feeling disappointed that they couldn't give birth in the usual way.

Some mothers even feel like a failure as a result, and, while having a C-section is certainly not a failure – babies are a joy and a delight regardless of the method that brought them into the world – such feelings are natural and normal, and will take time to overcome and deal with.

And, of course, besides the emotional effects of Caesarean section, there is also the physical side to consider; after all, the procedure involves major abdominal surgery that will take a number of weeks to recover from. Thankfully, your healthcare specialist will help you get through this physical recovery (including keeping you in hospital for a number of days after your baby has been delivered).

There are a number of natural solutions and remedies that can help you to cope with the feelings of disappointment and failure. Top of the list, however, is for mum and baby to have plenty of contact – cuddles, kisses, nursing, and so on. This really does help to relieve some of those unhelpful emotions, releasing positive hormones that help you to bond with your new baby and relax.

NATURAL SOLUTIONS AND REMEDIES

▶▶ HOMEOPATHY

Following a C-section, many women may feel a loss of control, shock and become very withdrawn and tearful, after such a major procedure. Homeopaths suggest taking Arnica 6c to help stabilize hormones and emotions and Aconite 6c for the shock of the delivery and birth.

▶▶ HERBAL REMEDIES

Valerian root is best known for its calming effects, being used in connection with feelings of sadness, nervousness and related conditions. This is the ideal herb to take when feeling disappointed after an emergency C-section, to balance the feelings of sadness and regret at not being able to have a natural birth.

▶▶ REFLEXOLOGY

Reflexology can help to balance your hormones and emotions after an emergency C-section by working on the pituary gland (master of all hormones) to help you relax and regain your body's balance and well-being.

▶▶ FLOWER REMEDIES

If you're feeling tearful or highly emotional, flower remedies such as Pine or Elm may bring relief in a gentle way.

▶▶ AROMATHERAPY

A healing aromatherapy bath once a day with the essential oils of rose otto and lavender (2 drops of each) will help to lift your mood and also help your wound to heal more quickly.

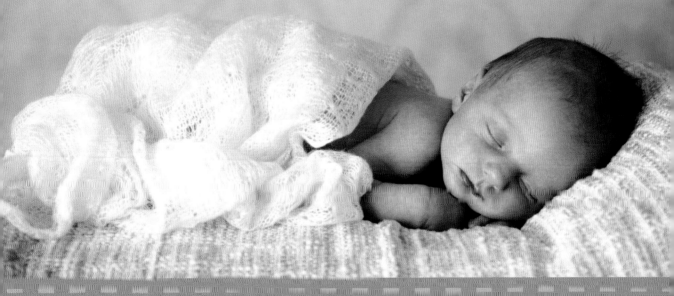

Stretch marks

Since the skin of your abdomen is rapidly stretched to many times its normal size, it's unsurprising that the majority of pregnant women develop stretch marks. These are narrow, red lines of scar tissue that arise during pregnancy and, after the baby is born, they fade to become thin, silvery lines that, in most cases, don't disappear.

Many women become very conscious of them, and so become embarrassed about their bodies. The vast range of creams, lotions, laser treatments and 'miracle cures' for stretch marks is testimony to this, but unfortunately most do not produce any lasting effect – and some have actually been known to cause irritation to the delicate skin around the abdomen. The good news is that there are also a number of natural ways you can help reduce the effect of stretch marks that will not cause you damage in return.

NATURAL SOLUTIONS AND REMEDIES

▶▶ HEALTHY FOODS
Eating may seem an odd way to deal with stretch marks – after all, it was the stretching of the skin around your belly that caused the marks in the first place – but there are a number of foods that can help to heal damaged skin tissue and encourage new growth. Eat foods that are rich in proteins, together with those containing vitamins C, E and K, and zinc. Nuts, for example, are good for stretch marks, as are seeds, dairy products, leafy vegetables, tomatoes and liver.

▶▶ EXERCISE
There is nothing like toning up your abdominal muscles to help your skin firm up. Avoid focusing solely on sit-ups and crunches, though; a good, all-round workout is one of the best remedies for stretch marks, as it helps to promote that all-important core strength.

▶▶ ALOE VERA
The leaves of this succulent plant contain an excellent skin moisturizer and healer, which is why it is found in so many skin care products. Straight off the plant is best, but if you don't have access to one there are plenty of aloe vera gels available, and all you need to do is apply it directly on the stretch marks at least once a day. It is fairly sticky at first but it does dry, and, as it does so, its enzymes help to

encourage the replacement of damaged skin tissue and counteract the effects of the stretch marks.

▶▶ ESSENTIAL OILS

The number one oil recommended for stretch marks is lavender, closely followed by tea tree oil. Lavender oil should be applied three times a day to the area in question, preferably starting as early as the second trimester – though should be avoided in the first. It is best used with a carrier oil such as chamomile, avocado, sweet almond or jojoba, all of which also help the skin's healing process. Tea tree oil is a natural 'scar healer' and is best applied once a day.

▶▶ COCOA BUTTER

Cocoa butter can be used during pregnancy to help keep stretch marks from developing as your bump grows. If you massage it into the relevant areas for a few minutes, twice a day, this will not only soften your skin, helping to retain its elasticity, but will also encourage good circulation, which helps to keep your skin in good shape.

EXTRA-STRENGTH HOME REMEDY

For more pronounced stretch marks, it may be necessary to combine certain oils with vitamins for the maximum effect. Try mixing avocado, lavender and chamomile oils with the contents of vitamin A and E capsules, for an effective home remedy.

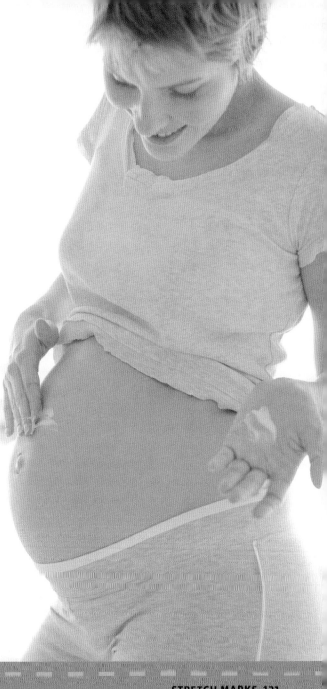

Sleep deprivation

It will come as no surprise that the most common ailment suffered by new mothers is sleep deprivation. Having a newborn, or even several-month-old, baby makes a good night's sleep unlikely.

Babies can be settled into a routine fairly quickly, ensuring their main sleep occurs at night, but you are guaranteed at least a few nights with less sleep than is ideal. When this happens, it's important to be on the lookout for signs that you might be suffering from sleep deprivation. These symptoms can become fairly extreme, and can even become a safety issue for you and your baby if they affect your balance and co-ordination.

There are a number of straightforward, natural ways to help counter the effects of sleep deprivation, and it's worth trying them all to see which work best for you.

NATURAL SOLUTIONS AND REMEDIES

➡ SET A BABY ROUTINE

It can be very tempting to let your days and nights be dictated by your baby's needs. However, there are a number of recommended routines that can help your baby settle into a pattern that is best for both of you (see pages 20–24 and 62–5). Using a routine will ensure your baby sleeps through the night as soon as possible, allowing you to access the best cure for sleep deprivation: a good night's sleep!

SYMPTOMS OF SLEEP DEPRIVATION INCLUDE:

- Being disorientated – especially if you've been woken during 'dream sleep'
- Impaired co-ordination and balance
- Feeling emotional and tearful for no obvious reason
- Becoming angry and irritable even with seemingly insignificant things
- Simply being tired and worn out

➡ NAPS AND EARLY NIGHTS

Since you are losing out on sleep during the night, it's important to try to make up for this when the opportunity arises. Napping while your baby is asleep during the day can really make a difference, but it does mean overcoming the urge to use that 'free time' for other things, such as catching up on jobs around the house or chatting with friends. Try to avoid this urge in the evenings as well, when your baby has settled down to sleep; as with napping, this is an ideal opportunity to get some much needed sleep – after all, who knows how soon you'll be having to get up again?

➡ WATCH WHAT YOU EAT

Try to avoid the temptation to eat or drink foods that contain sugar or caffeine. While sugar can give you a boost, it soon presents its bill and leaves you feeling more tired and drained than before. And, although caffeine can help to keep you awake, its

effects can last for up to
ten hours, which could make
it harder getting to sleep at night.

Good foods to counter sleep deprivation
are those that release energy slowly and consistently
during the day. These include wholemeal bread,
cereals, fruit, vegetables, eggs and fish. You might
want to add some iron-rich food to your diet as
well, to counter iron deficiency, which is common
after childbirth and exacerbates the effects of sleep
deprivation. Finally, drink plenty of water to ensure
you avoid the loss of energy that comes from even
mild dehydration.

⯈ SUPPORT

It's not a failure to admit that you are tired, and
finding it difficult to be a mum as a result. Sharing
how you're feeling with your partner or close friends,
and asking them for help and support so you can
get some rest, will hopefully mean you get some
downtime to recover. You will then be better able
to care for your baby.

If you're suffering from sleep deprivation, it's
also crucial not to take on additional active tasks or
responsibilities. Instead of going out to the shops,
for instance, consider doing your shopping online.
Or, if you have older children who aren't getting as
much of your attention as you might wish, rather
than doing extra activities with them, try giving
them some hugs or letting them watch television
in bed with you, giving them quality time while
also allowing yourself the rest your body needs.

RESOURCES

For Samantha's own blog, natural homemade remedies, recipes and advice, visit:

The Natural Baby Care Expert
www.thenaturalbabycareexpert.co.uk

Below are some other useful websites for new parents:

Association of Breastfeeding Mothers
Help and support with breastfeeding
www.abm.me.uk

Association for Post Natal Illness
Help and support for mums with PND
apni.org

Australian Breastfeeding Association
Support and education on breastfeeding
www.breastfeeding.asn.au

BabyWearing Institute
Find your local BabyWearing consultant (USA & Canada)
www.babywearingschool.com

Babywearing International
Babywearing help and advice
www.babywearinginternational.com

BirthChoiceUK
Information on birthing choices in the UK
www.birthchoiceuk.com

Bliss
The premature-baby charity
www.bliss.org.uk

Breastfeeding Inc.
Articles and resources from Dr Jack Newman and Edith Kernerman
www.breastfeedinginc.ca

Breastfeeding Network
Help and support with breastfeeding
www.breastfeedingnetwork.org.uk

Breastfeeding USA
Information and support
www.breastfeedingusa.org

Contact a Family
Information, advice and support for parents of children with special needs
www.cafamily.org.uk

Cry-sis
Support for parents with crying and sleepless children
www.cry-sis.org.uk

DAD.info
Information and support for fathers
www.dad.info

DBL
The Dunstan Baby Language system
www.dunstanbaby.com

Full Time Mothers
Campaigning group supporting the rights of full-time mums
www.fulltimemothers.org

Gingerbread
Support for single parent families
www.gingerbread.org.uk

HomeDad
Information and support for full-time dads
www.homedad.org.uk

International Association of Infant Massage (IAIM)
Offers First Touch Program courses for parents in Australia
www.iaim.org.au

La Leche League International
Support and advice for breastfeeding mothers worldwide
www.llli.org

Multiples of America
For parents of twins or more
www.nomotc.org

National Childbirth Trust
Charity and national network (UK) providing information, advice, classes and support from pregnancy to parenthood
www.nct.org.uk

Natural Parenting
Parenting support, directory and discussion forums (Australia)
www.naturalparenting.com.au

Post and Antenatal Depression Association Inc. (PANDA)
Support for parents in Australia
www.panda.org.au

Postpartum Support International (PSI)
Support for postnatal depression (worldwide)
www.postpartum.net

Reflux Infants Support Association Inc. (RISA)
Support for families of infants who suffer from reflux
www.reflux.org.au

Solace for Mothers
Support for mothers suffering from birth trauma
www.solaceformothers.org

INDEX

ACKNOWLEDGEMENTS

I would like to dedicate Comfort, Settle & Sleep to my three lovely children, Ella, Yasmin and Max. I love you to the moon and back. I would also like to make special acknowledgement to the following people:

To my husband Sam, for supporting me through all my goals and dreams. To my parents, who gave me more than I realized – thank you for all your support throughout my life. To my friends Lydia and Michelle, for our great friendship. To my Gran, who is no longer with us but I miss her every day. You would have been so proud of me; you always told me I could do anything. I just wish you were here to share it with me.

To my family, I am so lucky to have you, especially Nan, Granddad Peter, Granddad Fred, Rachel, Bob, Uncle Gavin, Uncle Paul, June, Karen and Billy. Thank you for supporting me and believing in me every step of the way – and to all my other family and friends who have made a difference in my life.

To all the wonderful mothers and babies I have taught throughout the years, you have all taught me so much. I am so grateful you gave me the experience I needed to write this book.

To Connections Book Publishing, thank you for bringing my book to life.

Thanks to Dunstan Baby Pty Ltd, for their kind permission to include the DBL information in chapter 1.

PICTURE CREDITS

The following abbreviations have been used throughout the picture credits: t top; b bottom; l left; r right

Cover ShutterStockphoto, Inc. – Vitalinka (front) / FamVeld (back); Nicki Feltham (back flap)

iStockphoto 4–5, 12, 14, 15, 18, 19, 21, 23, 25 42tr, 43tl, 53r, 54, 58t, 60t, 65tl, 72, 73, 85, 88–89, 99, 101, 103, 105, 107, 108,109, 110, 113, 121

ShutterStockphoto, Inc. albinutza 11; aldegonde 86–87; alekso94 106; Subbotina Anna 67; margo black 102; Nina Buday 37, 41; Nadezda Cruzova 32, 119; enieni 7; Tiplyashina Evgeniya 31; FamVeld 95; Sanit Fuangnakhon 91; Artem Furman 40; JetKat 62; jfk image 112; Evgeny Karandaev 82; Kiefer Pix 48t; Denis Kukareko 78; Oksana Kuzmina 93; Langstrup 28–29; Lerche&Johnson 98; Ilike 49r; luckyraccoon 9, 100; Sokolova Maryna 13; Svetlana Mihailova 82–83; Irena Misevic 96; MitarArt 94; MJTH 16; Dmitry Naumov 42tc, 43tr, 48br; An Nguyen 111; oksix 6; Khoroshunova Olga 27; Alena Ozerova 36, 45bl, 47; M.Unal Ozmen 116; Ana Blazic Pavlovic 22; Photobac 81; Praisaeng 61t, 65bl; Alina Reynbakh 90; Ivan Sabo 74; SailanaLT 30; Alexander Sayenko 50–51; Eugene Sergeev 75; SW Stock 76–77; Takayuki 70; Gladskikh Tatiana 66; Iryna Tiumentseva 48bl, 49tl, 64; Anastasia Tveretinova 97; Ventura 33; Windu 84; Olena Zaskochenko 79

Thinkstock Fuse 2–3; Ingram Publishing 42l; iStockphoto 26

Rebekah Grace 43tc, 45tr, 46, 47tr, 49bl, 50l, 51, 52, 53tl & bl, 55, 56, 57, 58br, 59, 60bl & br, 61b

EDDISON•SADD EDITIONS

Creative Director Nick Eddison
Managing Editor Tessa Monina
Proofreader Katie Golsby
Indexer Marie Lorimer
Designer Jane McKenna
Picture research administration Rosie Taylor
Production Sarah Rooney

Mumma Love Organics is Samantha's own award-winning natural skincare company. She is passionate about helping new mothers calm, soothe and comfort their babies.

Her natural range of products includes organic oils and balms designed with her three core principles at heart: Comfort, Settle and Sleep.

All of her products are organic, midwife-approved, British-made and specially formulated to leave baby feeling calm, confident and happy.

For more information, and to order products online, visit **www.mummaloveorganics.com**